"If you board a random aircraft every day, statistically, it will take 26,000 years before you would be involved in a major airline accident—even then you might survive"—**Unbekannt**

"A fully loaded Boeing 727 would have to crash every day of the year to equal the annual number of car fatalities"—**Inconnu**

"You must demand excellence"—**Juan Terry Trippe**

"I could see that there was less competition abroad than at home"—**Juan Terry Trippe**

"I got vision while the rest of the world wears bifocals"—**Butch Cassidy**...but could just as well have been Juan Trippe

"One memorable trip was in 1949. We went to Paris for Christmas and on to Switzerland for a family ski trip. In Paris, Dad met with General Eisenhower on Christmas Eve and tried to convince him to become the Republican candidate for President"—**Ed Trippe**

ABOUT THE AUTHOR

JON BREAKFIELD is the author of six books. These include the non-fiction bestsellers *KEY WEST*, the sequel *KEY WEST Part II*, the eye-popping adventure *NAKED EUROPE* and his Scottish bestselling crime-thriller *DEATH BY GLASGOW* (which was shortlisted for the 2012 Crime Writers' Association's Debut Dagger Award), and the stand-alone sequel *DEATH BY KEY WEST*.

He and his wife divide their time between the historic Horseshoe Bar in Glasgow, Scotland, and the bacchanal Bull & Whistle Bar in Key West, Florida.

PAN AM

(No Sex Please, We're Flight Attendants)

by

Jon Breakfield

PAN AM copyright © 2016 Jon Breakfield
All rights reserved
First published in the United States of America by Key West Press. Published in the United Kingdom by Gallowgate Press. No part of this book may be used or reproduced in any manner without written permission except in the case of brief quotations embodied in critical articles, reviews, and on the walls of airport toilets around the world.
Jon Breakfield has asserted his right under the Copyright, Designs and Patent Act 1988 to be identified as the author of this work.
www.JonBreakfield.com
Cover design Key West Press
KEY WEST PRESS and the Key West Press colophon are registered trademarks

In Memory of Carrie Thomas (Class Four, 1973), and Vigdis Gjesdal (Class Three, 1973)

ACKNOWLEDGEMENTS: A round-the-world shout-out (and a raised glass) to Stanford Oliver, Diane Roberts, Muffy Harmar, Chris Curtiss, Rob Halkides, Wendy Shepherd, Anna-Lise Schwartz, Janie Hulton, Roye Miller, Corolla, Siobhan, Bella, Zelda, and the rest of the Pan Am family

My editor GLB

And I must not forget Captain Tom Weller, British Airways, an international beer taster and fellow skier

CONTENTS

1. Wind Shear
2. Kano, Nigeria
3. A Man Down a Dark Alley
4. An Airplane Has a Certain Smell, *usually*
5. Bat Strikes
6. The Lebanese Club
7. Disease, Hunger, and the Basque Country
8. Swedish Squeals on the Train to Frankfurt
9. My First Interview, Yikes…
10. Training School Begins
11. Terror in the Classroom
12. The Best Airline in the World
13. A Young Boy
14. Lineage
15. But First, *Radio*
16. A Difficult Birth
17. You Have to Make Your Own Luck
18. In-Flight
19. Drunk with the Spectre of Sex

20 Graduation, and Off to London

21 My First Flight!

22 Caught Between a Hard Rock and Home

23 New Uniforms, *sadly*

24 Once, There Were Only Stewards

25 And You, Sir, POOOFFF! You Are a Wee Piece of Shite!

26 An Unwelcomed Visitor

27 *Encore à* Beirut

28 Left to Rot in Beirut

29 New Delhi

30 Maiming Children

31 Do Not Attempt to Land!

32 A Delicate Situation

33 A Good Night for a Ditching

34 Not Allowed to Project Fatigue

35 The Worst News Possible

36 I Travel to Tenerife

37 A Change in the Air, and a Chill

EPILOGUE

1

Wind Shear!

"Ladies and gentlemen, we will be arriving at Miami International Airport in just a few minutes. At this time we ask that you bring your seatbacks forward, make sure your tray tables are in an upright position, ensure that all cabin bags are stowed underneath the seat in front of you or in the overhead bins, and that your seatbelts are securely fastened. Thank you."

The aircraft banked. I peered out the window but couldn't see anything except dark menacing clouds. Towering thunderheads had been forecast for our arrival and the forecasters were right for once. Lightning was striking all around us.

The plane was on final approach, descending lower and lower, when it began to sway back and forth. Side to side. A motion that normally would lull a person to sleep, but not tonight. Not in this tropically restive weather.

Lower we came. Still lower. Not long now. Seconds from touchdown. That cushion of air. Suddenly a jolt. Then another. And WHOOSH! the aircraft dropped out of the sky and SLAMMED the ground with a horrifying splitting sound.

Wind shear! my mind yelled out. We were skidding off the runway now. People were screaming for their lives. There was panic.

But I knew what I had to do.

I was the flight attendant positioned near the aft exit on the right-hand side. The minute we thudded to a stop, I peeked out through my exit door's little round window. "FIRE!" I yelled to my colleague across the aisle. With fire outside, my exit was rendered useless. If I opened the door and deployed the escape slide, the fire would be sucked in and we would all die a horrific death.

Passengers seated in the back of the plane, now stricken with fear, rushed toward us. They wanted out. I shot to the other side of the cabin where my colleague was struggling with her exit door.

"Fire?"

"No fire, but it won't open!"

I jerked on the handle, dipped a shoulder and hit it with everything I had. Nothing. I hit it again. Jammed! Desperate passengers pushed and shoved up against us. There was no escape out the aft section of the aircraft.

Suddenly there was smoke in the cabin.

"Turn around! We have to go back!" I yelled. "These exits are blocked!"

But the passengers were frozen in place.

"Turn around! Go back!" the petite flight attendant yelled.

No one moved.

Like enraged bulls, we forced the backs of seats forward and the two of us hurdled the folded seats.

"C'mon! Follow us! Climb over the back of the seats like we are!" It was the only way to unplug the blocked aisle.

All the passengers who had been trapped in the burning aft section of the aircraft followed us, clattering over the folded seats, and we guided them out an already open over-wing exit. Finally, making sure no one else was in the aircraft, we too leaped out into fresh air and down to the ground. Much to our surprise standing there in front of me where a wing should have been was a silver-haired gentleman holding a stopwatch.

"Sixty-eight seconds," said the examiner, stopping the watch. "Well done, everyone!"

What you just read above happened inside a mock-up during my Emergency Week at Pan Am Training School in Miami: sound effects and fake smoke and a shuddering "fuselage" had made it all frighteningly real. And that training exercise sprang into my mind every time we took off or landed. I couldn't help it. "Emergency Week" in Training School had scared the bejesus out of us all.

2

Kano, Nigeria

And years later, I still had Emergency Week on the brain as our Pan Am Boeing 747 screamed down the runway in Kano, Nigeria, narrowly missing the "honey wagon" taking an ill-advised shortcut across the runway to the terminal.

A bladder-challenging nanosecond passed. The wailing Pratt & Whitney engines generated unimaginable thrust. Then, without warning, the massive piece of machinery defied gravity and, like a coiled serpent, suddenly sprang into the pre-dawn sky.

We hung seemingly motionless for a fleeting instant and I wondered for a split second as I always did if the airplane would soar upwards as a great bird or unceremoniously fall out of the sky and send us to a fiery death where polyurethane foam seat cushions burn like napalm in a 1000C inferno.

I white-knuckled, and just when I thought everything was going to be okay, something decidedly peculiar happened: the aircraft rotated and a wave of fetid urine, two-inches deep, started to roll slowly back through the cabin like a gentle breaker at Waikiki. As if on cue, the hundreds of Nigerian passengers sitting in front of me started chanting a surprisingly catchy primordial chant.

"The hell's going on?!" I yelled over to Bella, the flight attendant sitting across from me at R5, the other aft exit.

Bella was a spunky Mackam from the northeast of England, with a retroussé nose and contorted patois, and she was laughing condescendingly at me. "Hold ya gob, Breakfield. Whaddye expect a first-class skive to Rio? In five hours that canny little backside of yours is going to be buggered from cleaning up these jangos' shite."

"Is that the Queen's English?"

Bella gave me the two-fingered Agincourt salute.

Even though Bella was a royal pain, I couldn't help noticing she had killer legs as she held them up in the air so the pee wouldn't soak her shoes.

"Stop looking at me legs and lift up yours, ye wanker! Lift up your legs so these gadjis divint go pissing all over your poofter shoes!" Bella squirmed in her seat as if her knickers were in a serious twist. "Is this your first hajj?"

"Yes."

"Sod's Law. Just what ah need, a lad who's still in nappies. If owt goes wrong, there's bugger all ye can do about it, bonnie lad." Bella lifted her legs higher, and her skirt went halfway up to her panties. "Ahh, ye first timers!"

As a vile stench wafted around us, I lifted my legs up in the air like Bella, and because I hadn't understood anything Bella had said up until now, I simply yelled, "I don't remember anything about this in Training School. I don't remember anything about this at all!"

No, they didn't say anything in Flight Attendant Training School about holding your feet up in the air like a Ringling Brothers' contortionist until the plane leveled off. Nor did they say anything about Mecca, the hajj, and transporting primitive bush people who lived in mud huts and whose world was so culturally distant from my own they urinated in their seats, in the aisles, or on the bulkheads of the cabin because they had never seen a lavatory. One pilgrim used sign language to convey that he desperately needed the toilet. "See that door right back there?" I said, pointing and miming. The man gave me a rescued smile, walked up to the door and peed on it.

* * *

Fifteen hours later, I was sitting in the bar at our layover hotel in Kano, knocking back a rather fetching tall green bottle of "Star lager." It was two in the morning. I looked around the bar. Just me and the barkeep. The bar had large double doors which opened out onto the pool area. They were kept open to give us a breath of fresh air, and make it easier for the mosquitos to find us. The entire setting was dark and moody, sinister even. The type of place you wouldn't go in if you were paying for it yourself. The décor was somewhere between old colonial and suspect taste. "Watermelon" art, carved from real watermelons, on all the tables and sideboards. Broad leafy plants endeavouring to hide hideously green walls. All the furniture from a bygone era and now chipped and tired. Ceiling fans circling ineffectually overhead. It was hot, 97 degrees with debilitating humidity, and the air smelled of wood burning somewhere. Somewhere right out there in the bush.

This was not the luxury class of hotel I had come to know while flying with Pan Am. Our layover hotels were traditionally some of the finest five-star hotels in the world, and now here I was drinking a beer that had more stars than our hotel.

Behind the bar pouring the drinks was "Franky." He made it all worthwhile. He looked like Satchmo, face glistening with perspiration, lots of very white teeth, and he laughed at everything. *Everything.*

"Hi."

Laughter from Franky.

"What's your name?"

"Franky."

Laughter.

"Franky?"

Laughter.

"My name's Jon."

Laughter.

It was hard not to like Franky.

I took a good long pull on my Star lager. Had I really been through "hajj hell" and back? Five-hour flight up to Jeddah, Saudi Arabia, two, yes you heard right *two*, excruciating, life-sucking hours deplaning our very confused, first-time flyers, one more hour waiting for Immigration to make an appearance to stamp a lonely document, another vexing hour waiting for Customs to arrive so they could check an empty, piss-riddled aircraft, lest we be smuggling something into Saudi Arabia (like human rights), ten minutes spraying the aircraft for airborne creepy crawlies, five hours ferrying an empty aircraft teeming with pissed-off, airborne, evolutionary stalwarts back to home base, then God knows how long waiting in the dark and the heat watching a shiny limo pick up the cockpit crew, while awaiting our ramshackle, creaking-and-groaning crew bus to eventually arrive and whisk us away to salvation.

The hajj was, and perhaps I should just whisper this so as not to offend, turning us all to alcohol, and we felt sincerely blessed that our hotel was one of the few *in the very dry city* of Kano that served liquor.

Our hotel was just one of the watering holes, then there was the famous and naughty Lebanese Club, and the seedy and dangerous bush bars. I wanted to go to a bush bar, but Franky warned against it and said in his broken English something which amounted to: "Don't even think about it. Even during the day. They are always located down dark lanes. The establishments will not impress. There will be a floor with just bare earth, there may be a few lanterns hanging from a tree overhead. They are a haunt of criminals. You could end up hanging in the tree next to the lanterns. You will not be welcome and they will let you know it."

Comparable to stepping into a pub in north Wales and not speaking Welsh?

Or a pub on the wrong side of the river in Glasgow sporting the wrong colours?

* * *

One by one, other beleaguered crew members from the trip dragged their weary carcasses into the bar and pulled up a chair next to me. Sleep was coveted, but alcohol was even higher on the list of priorities after a tough round-trip flight. I'm not saying we were a bunch of drunks (that honour was held by British Airways cockpit crews), but there was something special about unwinding with your colleagues and recounting the events of the day or previous trips.

Bella was the first to make an appearance. She didn't seem the type who would miss the chance to knock back the plonk.

My eyes bulged as Bella swept in. She was sex on wheels, all plunging, all decamping.

From behind the transom, I heard laughter.

On account of the constant threat of malaria, I was wearing long sleeves and long trousers despite the heat. Bella was wearing some exotic wrap around, tropical, serape sort of thing that left very little to the imagination. It was always enlightening to be on a layover and see the other cabin attendants out of their uniforms and into the clothes that defined their non-Pan Am persona. It said so much about them. It was almost like reading their DNA.

Franky approached, laughing, and Bella ordered the Nigerian equivalent of a Screaming Orgasm. I think it was called a "Lagos Leg Over," but I may have been mistaken.

Soon after, Bernie the flight engineer arrived. He, too, was wearing long sleeves and long trousers. He ordered a Star lager, from laughing Franky. Then came Sieglinda from Germany. Sieglinda had the longest legs I had ever seen on a woman, and they were featured in something I could only describe as borrowed from the musical *Hair* (just before the lights were dimmed and the cast flashed the audience). Soon after Carina from Scotland entered and Leslie from England. They were dressed conservatively against the mozzies. Sieglinda ordered a Star lager, and Carina and Leslie hit the hard stuff. I had the distinct feeling I was amongst professional drinkers. Everyone was more senior than I was and they all had worked the hajj before out of Tehran, but this was the first time for them flying out of Kano.

Bella lapped at her evil looking concoction, and leaned over to me. "How'd you swing the hajj, bonnie lad? You're not very senior."

I slapped at a mosquito and applied more insect repellent. "I was told I was too junior to try for it. I figured everyone else would be thinking they were too junior, as well, and wouldn't try. So I tried."

"And you got it."

"I got it."

"That sort of twisted logic always serve you well, bonnie lad?"

"Actually, it has."

"Well, I was supposed to be doing the hajj in Tehran," Bella said, "staying at the five-star Hilton or InterContinental, not here in the arse end of Nigeria staying at the Bates Motel. I do believe we got the proverbial royal shaft."

"You may have, I didn't."

"What are you saying?"

"I'm saying I'm really enjoying being here."

Bella rolled her eyes at me.

Bernie apparently was known for his great stories and it didn't take long before he launched into one of them.

"Had a flight into Lagos a few years back. Flying a seven-four. We were arriving in the middle of the night. It was never dull, Lagos, as you could count on many of the landing lights being out. Anyhoo, we came in over the ocean, over the houseboats and the floating slums, and we had bird strikes. Just before we touched down, we saw locals scurrying across the runway taking a shortcut to get to the terminal. Crazy bastards. No gates for us, so we taxied to a remote area, shut the engines down. The captain and I did a walk around to see if there was any damage from the bird strikes..."

Bernie knocked back his beer and motioned to Franky for another.

"Well, no damage from the bird strikes, but we did find something."

All of us leaned forward in our seats. I glanced over at Franky. He was riveted.

"In a wheel-well, we found a teenage boy who had just climbed up in there."

"What was he thinking?" Bella asked.

"Pan Am. We represented a way out of whatever Godforsaken hell-hole he was living in."

Bernie's Star lager arrived. Franky was not laughing.

Bernie sucked on his lager. Reliving that night. "The boy wouldn't come down. We got the police on the horn and they came and dragged him down out of there. They beat him. Right there in front of us. Our captain interceded with: "My airplane! My jurisdiction!" The police stopped beating the boy and locked eyes with the captain. Had a bit of tug-a-war. "My airplane," the captain repeated. One of the police said: "No report." And they let the boy go. He ran back off across the runway. Jesus. You just never know what's going to happen in the back of beyond."

Not much later, Bella and I watched Bernie as he let go with what seemed like a theatrical yawn.

"Think I'll turn in," Bernie intoned. He rose, bid us all goodnight, and scarpered, a bit too eager to hit the sheets. Weren't cockpit crews meant to close the bar? Wasn't it in their contract?

Within minutes, Carina let go with a fake yawn and departed.

I looked over at Bella and held both palms up.

"They're doing it," Bella hissed. "Lucky sods."

"Are they an item?"

"Tonight they are."

I ordered another beer and Bella ordered another evil, screaming concoction. While we were waiting for our drinks to come, Bella squirted some of my insect repellent across her bare neck and swabbed down the tops of her breasts.

She caught me looking again. "Why did you join the airline, bonnie lad, let me guess." She held both hands to her forehead as a swami would. "You'd heard there weren't many male cabin attendants and you thought it would be like shooting fish in a tub..."

"Huh?"

"Shooting fish in a *barrel*. Piece of cake. Get with the program."

I laughed. I was slowly learning that Bella wasn't always being rude, she just had a different, wickedly sarcastic sense of humour to the type I had grown up with.

"Yes, it had crossed my mind that there would be a lot of available women working with the airlines, but that wasn't the real reason. I like languages and I like far-off places."

"Never heard that one before."

"What *have* you heard?"

"Well, for many of us girls…looking for men with money…"

"Mr. Right?"

"If he's got lots of dosh, then aye bonnie lad, that would make him Mr. Right."

I gave this some thought. If many of the female cabin attendants were in the hunt for the big bucks, nary a one would have any interest in me. Although, in saying that, there was always overtime and per diem…

Our drinks arrived and it was now Bella, Sieglinda and Leslie's turn to tell airline stories. It was often like this, talking about Pan Am all the time. Telling airline stories all the time. But some flight attendants didn't partake. "Can't you talk about anything else other than Pan Am?" Oddly, the response was often a simple "No." Talking about Pan Am meant talking about adventure, sex, practical jokes, bizarre passengers, the four corners of the earth, exotic layovers—and the inherent dangers that came with flying.

Bella was the most senior of us, and she was the first to hold sway.

"When I was based in San Francisco, we had a rather heavyset man die on the way back from Shanghai. No surprise as he looked like a walking heart attack. He was seated in the back of the aircraft…"

"How'd you know he was dead?" Leslie asked.

"Oh, when you see one you'll know," Bella said. "His eyes were open. Quite creepy. We didn't know what to do. It was the middle of the night and he had his reading light on. The purser informed the captain, and the captain told us that usually we would make an announcement and ask if there was a doctor or nurse onboard. That, plus, we should be giving CPR for the rest of the flight. Remember in Training School, we have to administer CPR and can't stop, because stopping means we are pronouncing the passenger dead, and only a medical doctor can do that."

Bella stopped for a moment and hit her drink hard.

"You won't believe what we did, we didn't have a 'corpse cupboard' like Singapore Airlines, so the captain told us to do what had happened on another Pan Am flight: 'Turn off his reading light, put eye shades on him, pull a blanket up around his neck and stick a drink in front of him on the tray table'."

Sieglinda guffawed, Germans live for *Schadenfreude*.

But the rest of us were horrified.

Bella carried on. "The reason I recount this wee story is that the following year we had two trainees onboard, one male, one female. We were operating a New York to London. A light load. Empty in the back. Middle of the night. We went up to the male trainee, a young, bit full-of-himself English lad from the Cotswolds. He had been stuck in First Class and was a star-struck, dribbling wreck on account of David Niven being up front. We informed the trainee that a passenger at the rear of the aircraft had died. We led him to the back and he could just make out a man in the back row wearing eye shades, with a blanket pulled up around his neck, a drink on the tray table in front of him. We told the trainee that rules dictated that a crew member had to sit next to the deceased. It was protocol. The trainee said he didn't remember anything about dead people in Training School and was none too keen to take up his position, but he did as he was instructed."

Bella threw down the rest of her drink. And, looking right at me, sucked enthusiastically on the straw.

Foreplay?

"After about fifteen minutes, with the trainee steward a tightly wound spring, the corpse turned to him and politely asked: 'Do you mind if I smoke?' The trainee almost had a stroke. The 'corpse' was the aft purser. We laughed our arses off all the way into Heathrow."

We laughed, as well, then Bella rose and headed off toward her *single* room. She landed the single room because she was the most senior, and the odd one out. She stopped, looked back, beckoned, whispered my name: "Jon." Lots of subtext.

Loads of sexual innuendo.

I perked up. Hope springs eternal, doesn't it? I scurried over to her: "Yes? Yes?"

"Don't forget to take your malaria pill."

* * *

Soon after, Sieglinda and Leslie were a concerto of gaping yawns, and they wobbled off to the room they were sharing. I went outside by the pool and hung out with a gecko, but the mosquitoes were in mid-season form, so I went back into the bar and admired the watermelon art and talked to Franky. Franky had been the barman at the hotel for thirty years. And he loved it.

"I like people," he said. "I used to work at prison in Kano. Job okay, but conditions not so okay. Lot people sick. Lot people sad. Make Franky unhappy. Franky think he can change. Make people happy. Guards beat prisoners. Not good. I come here. Good."

"Good," I said.

And Franky laughed.

"Not many hotels serve alcohol in Kano. Are you okay with that?"

"Yes, residents only. No locals."

I talked with Franky a bit more, finally bid him goodnight and took what was left of my beer back to my room.

Our hotel was very basic. As I've alluded to, this was not the five-star palaces we were used to staying in like the Ashoka or Oberoi in Delhi, or the Phoenicia in Beirut, or the Siam Intercontinental in Bangkok, the Royal Hawaiian in Waikiki, or the Keio Plaza in Tokyo. This was a two-story, zippo-star with rumbling plumbing, cockroaches and resident voyeurs. Men with a lot of time on their hands were always milling about by the front entrance. Occasionally, one would penetrate the compound and sit by the swimming pool watching the stewardesses in bikinis until he was asked to leave.

I got to my room, then realized I wasn't at my room. The hotel was a compound with separate buildings and they all looked the same. Especially if you had been knocking back Star lager. Eventually I found the correct building. And the correct room. I inserted my key and opened the door. Sitting on one of the double beds, was my roommate. I did a double-take and wrinkled my nose.

"What's that awful smell?"

"Housekeeping was in spraying for bugs. Little good it does, I think the cockroaches live for it."

I studied my roommate. He was holding a bulging handkerchief. He spread the handkerchief open and displayed a deep-green, rich mound of what looked to be finely cut oregano.

"Want to get high?" he asked.

"Where'd you get that?"

"The houseboy?"

I think my jaw fell open. No wait, I *know* my jaw fell open. I took a long pull of my beer. "Are you nuts? You went up to a perfect stranger in a foreign country and asked him if he could score some drugs for you?"

"Right."

"How much did you pay for that?"

"Five dollars."

"For all that?"

My roommate stuck his nose in the mound of weed and inhaled deeply. "It's a great country!"

I studied my roommate again. Long and hard. We were both going to get thrown in the Kano, Hilton, where it was "sad and sick." And we'd be cellmates for life. My roommate's name was Juan. He was from Puerto Rico. "Juan from San Juan."

Cringe.

Juan had flown with Pan Am well past his shelf life and had been hired because he spoke Spanish, Portuguese, French, and a really curious strain of English. The job with Pan Am seemed to get in the way of his lifestyle. I should have known I was going to be in trouble with San-Juan Juan as a roommate. When he had been Miami based, and a purser (before he was demoted), he had freely told me, he could bring in as much as $500 extra a month by taking home the "miniatures," and refilling them with his own generic no-name supply of scotch, gin, rum and vodka. When he worked the economy section, the other flight attendants were always thankful that he "broke the seal" on the miniatures before he placed the bottles on the coded drinks tray. Only a few of the passengers questioned the difference in quality of the booze, and when they did, our Juan would just offer a freebie. And he delivered them himself, offering an apology and "breaking" the seal right in front of the offended passenger.

"I'm going for a walk," I said.

"Sure you don't want to get high?"

"I'm sure. Listen, Juan, I don't care what you do as long as it doesn't affect others, so do me a favor and get that stuff out of here."

* * *

I knocked on Bella's door. I waited. Nothing. I sipped my beer. I knocked again. Nothing. I walked over to her window and peered through the slats. I was going to get caught for being a Peeping Tom and get arrested and still thrown in the slammer with all the dodgy men who milled about out front of the hotel. No Bella. Where had she gone? I went back to the bar. The place was suddenly heaving. A Martinair crew was in. It was always easy to spot the other crews and no problem to figure which airline.

Franky was in his element.

I ordered another Star lager and paid with Naira. There was a bowl of funny looking nuts on the bar, next to some watermelon art. I desperately wanted to dip into the nuts, but you know about nuts in bars, don't you? Plus, I was leery about eating anything that was hanging around in the open. I couldn't imagine what it would be like to go to a hospital in Nigeria. With this in mind, I mostly ate on the plane. If it was fruit, I still washed the heck out of it and made sure I peeled it myself. Up until yesterday morning, I had felt toast would be okay. How can you mess up toast? I had ordered it at breakfast, then watched in horror as the waiter walked across the dining room, grabbed a plate of toast off a just-vacated table and placed it in front of me—with a smile.

* * *

I awoke with a start the next morning. I had fallen asleep on a chaise lounge out by the pool, and mosquitoes had feasted on me. Now I was going to get malaria AND go to jail. I looked around. An iguana was sitting nearby, sizing me up. I tried to stare him down, but I couldn't rotate my eyes like he could. I decided to go inside and get a coffee.

My coffee arrived and I sipped at it trying to get the cobwebs out. Out of the corner of my eye, I saw a figure approaching. It was San-Juan Juan.

"You score last night, amigo…or did you come in late? I passed out."

"I can believe you did. And, no, I didn't score. Did you get rid of it?"

"Hidden."

"Out of the room?"

"Yes…out of the room."

We were interrupted by Bobby, another male flight attendant, who just happened to be Nigerian. Bobby was self-professed *stunningly good-looking* and had spent most of his career based in San Francisco, and had never met a man he didn't fancy.

"I'm going into the Old City. Want to come along?"

I looked over at San-Juan Juan. Was Bobby talking to both of us?

"I'm going," San-Juan Juan said. He turned to me. "You coming, amigo? Bobby will be our tour guide…"

"Bobby's from the south, Lagos," I said, presenting my case. "Different accent, different culture, different religion…"

"So? You coming?"

"But there's curfews in some parts, the threat of terrorism, abductions…"

" So, you coming?"

"Off course I'm coming," I said.

Bobby, San-Juan Juan and I, hailed a cab from out front of our layover hotel. Once we hit the outskirts of Kano, the streets became clogged with sputtering "tuk-tuks," and motor scooters with *three* passengers, bicyclists with two passengers plus a small child, two-wheel water delivery wagons being pushed by hand, and the traffic slowed to somewhere between slow and dead-slow. It was scorching hot and we put all the windows down even though there was thick dust in the air, dust from the Sahara. I thought the dust was the famous "Harmattan haze," but Bobby informed me that the Harmattan-haze nightmare, where airlines have to be diverted and meningitis increases, is limited to the winter months. "And the temperature can drop to just 3 degrees Celsius, as the dust clouds nearly blot out the sun. The air becomes so dry, trees split."

The stench of car fumes and smoke from dung fires slapped us across the face. There were emaciated cows on the road and green street signs along the side of the road proclaiming "ALLAH IS THE GREATEST." And there were white, dented oil barrels being used as garbage containers with KEEP KANO CLEAN painted on the side in small, dirty letters.

We passed by a man selling spicy bush meat and goat meat. *Raw meat in this heat!* His "shop" was just two saw horses with a few boards on top, sitting on the corner of a dirt lot. There was no grass, but there was a canopy-like acacia tree. A few older men in full Nigerian dress sat on plastic chairs beneath the tree. The vendor had a little colourful umbrella, but it wasn't positioned correctly to protect the meat. Only the men. There was litter strewn about his business, a few burning logs and a filthy toddler playing next to it all. An air force of flies buzzed overhead. I noticed a 75cc, rusty motor bike parked out in front of his little business. Did he commute?

We motored past vast mounds of chili peppers being dried right out on the side of the road, and we saw a machine shop, of sorts, a cement-block, one-story structure with a corrugated tin roof where a few men worked in dusty conditions repairing what looked to be motors for refrigerators and the odd A/C unit. Wires snaked up from the ramshackle building to a nearby power pole.

The cabbie drove by a community water well where elderly women filled plastic containers and a few men washed, and eventually dropped us off in one of the most bustling sections of the city, then tried to extort double the fare. He shut up when Bobby gave him a tongue lashing in the local Hausa language. I was glad Bobby was with us.

"What did you say to him" I asked.

"Just told him what I'd do with his twins."

The minute we stepped from the taxi all eyes were on us.

"We're from mars," I said.

"Deeper in the universe," San-Juan Juan said.

I looked over at Bobby. He was immaculate and well-dressed. And he looked concerned.

"What is it, Bobby?"

"I'm Nigerian, but now I look like I'm *wealthy* Nigerian. I'm so a target for kidnap and ransom."

"Thanks for telling us in advance," San-Juan Juan said.

"Are there any safe areas in Kano?"

"Yes, indeed."

"Where?"

"How should I know? I'm from the south," Bobby said. He removed his gold watch from his wrist and put it in a pocket. San-Juan Juan removed his gold watch. Then I removed my Poo Bear watch. It was a big hit with the children on the plane.

When we flew with the airline, and had layovers in Beirut, we would go to Joe's Inter-Line in the gold market and make gold purchases. All of us did, males, females. We openly wore gold bracelets, necklaces and rings. It was fun to buy them and fun to wear them. They were our trophies that showed others we flew to exotic locals where such items were readily available and affordable. Back then gold was under one-hundred dollars an ounce.

Imagine.

I looked over at Bobby. He was dripping in more gold than Mr. T. used to wear. Same for San-Juan Juan, although a shorter version and without the Mohawk. I looked down at the 18-carat gold bracelet I wore on my left wrist. I fondled the gold chain with jaunty scimitar dagger hanging around my neck. Not good.

Bobby saw a policeman. He looked patently more dangerous than anyone we'd seen up till then. We approached and Bobby spoke to him in his native tongue. He wasn't expecting that. Bobby seemed to be asking directions. When Bobby was done, he grabbed us both by the elbow and led us away.

"What?"

"He said stay on the main streets. He said we really stand out."

We did as the policeman suggested and came across vendors flogging palm oil, then we saw what Bobby told us were young students begging for their meals. "They come from Chad, Niger and other parts of Nigeria. They come here to study the Koran, but they still need to beg for their meals."

Kano was dirty and had poor sanitation. And it had a sinister feel to it. And I have to say it again: It was hot and dusty and it stank. There were open fires on the street corners and more meat was being cooked right out in the open and offered for sale to the public. There were roving packs of straggly malnourished dogs, and we spent an inordinate amount of time looking over our shoulders, which made us stand out even more. There were rows of little stalls selling hot tea and steaming food and frankincense and saffron. We purchased some bottled water from a walking vendor, but San-Juan Juan noticed that the seals were broken, so we didn't drink. We passed stalls selling trinkets. At one stall, Bobby bought a full Nigerian outfit and haggled so vociferously, I thought he and the vendor would come to blows.

"Got a great deal!" Bobby said.

"Where will you wear that?"
"Back in San Fran."
"Fancy dress party?"
"No, just around the house."

Later, we entered a more modern section of Kano, and we didn't see any women anywhere. There were men loitering, smoking, talking among themselves. Talking about us.

Bobby studied the scene. "Not liking this. Let's catch a taxi back to the hotel before it gets dark."

We flagged down an approaching cab and couldn't believe what a rattle-trap it was. All three of us had to climb in the back as the driver had his young son sitting up front. This made us feel slightly better.

The taxi cut through what I took to be the downtown, then as we slipped toward the outskirts, we saw a roadblock up ahead, manned by the police. This was an unauthorized checkpoint, and the police tried to extort money from us. The cabbie tried to intervene, but Bobby silenced him. He spoke to the police firmly and directly.

And the police let us go.

"What did you say?"

"I said we worked for Pan Am and that put the fear of God in them."

Indeed, that's what it was like back then. If you were Pan Am, you were an unofficial ambassador representing the United States of America.

And it carried a great deal of weight.

3

A Man Down a Dark Alley

Later that evening, I was sitting in the bar with Bobby. We were trying to remember the "bottle to throttle" rule about how many hours we needed to abstain before our flight. Was it eight hours or was it twelve? In any case, we were doing our best to knock back as much beer as we could before the bewitching hour. We had asked San-Juan Juan to join us, but he said "he had other plans."

Bobby and I were telling "war stories." Perhaps it was because all of us at Pan Am were of similar ilk, no matter what your position with the airline or your personal persuasion, but often we would show a side of us to our workmates that we just wouldn't show to anyone outside of Pan Am. I think you know what I'm talking about here. Perhaps, not everyone and not on every flight, but enough over the course of our flying career to make us realize how special it all was, how close so many of us were, and how it is still that way to this day.

Perhaps family is too strong a word to use.

Perhaps it's not.

I was telling Bobby about a female cabin attendant I often flew with. She had confided in me. I didn't name names, but I did recount her story. This young lady had been trying to get with the airlines for quite some time. She interviewed with airline after airline, but never got hired. She was attractive, had a nice figure, was personable, intelligent, and spoke three languages. She was of the right height and the correct weight, had a smile that would light up a room, and had a college degree in nursing.

But nobody wanted her.

She was too old.

She was, shock/horror, 32 and even though she looked

22, no one would touch her. She was doomed by chronology. She wanted to fly. It was her dream. Her quest. Her every single cliché you could muster.

Then, one day she figured out how she could get hired. And not only hired, but hired by the best airline in the world—Pan American World Airways. She went to her father and told him of her plan. He didn't approve. She begged him and eventually he relented. Her father was a printer. He had contacts. He "knew a man."

She took the subway into Brooklyn, hustled down the proverbial dark alley. Knocked on a door and a week later, went back and knocked on the same door. When she came out this time, she came out with a new passport. A passport that listed her age as 22.

"Holy crap."

Bobby checked his watch and ordered two more beers.

I told Bobby about a flight I had from Beirut to London. "We had boarded about 30 religious zealots in Beirut. They had all been up to Baalbek and were in an agitated state. Thankfully they took up most of the yellow section, as they were just a bit off putting in their white robes and straggly beards. Sort of a cross between Charles Manson and Marilyn Manson.

"About an hour before we arrived in Istanbul, one of the devout suddenly 'saw the face of God' and became hysterical. Pan Am had always catered to celebrities, but this was more than anyone had ever anticipated. The believer became more and more hysterical, such was his joy, and he actually started to froth at the mouth. You can well understand the other passengers in the yellow section were not embracing the moment as were the rest of the religious zealots, who now were desperately trying to see the face of God on their own accord.

"None of us working in the back knew what to do, so we did what we always did when trouble erupted, we called the In-flight Director. The IFD was English and nothing ever seemed to faze her. She came to the back and observed the screaming, frothing believer, who was now on the floor between two rows. Pretty much the entire economy section was freaked out. The IFD did the only thing possible. It was a light load up front, so she stuck him up in First Class."

"What did the other First Class passengers do?"

"Nothing. There's often someone in First Class making a scene."

"Well, I can beat that…"

"Someone you know, personally?"

"Intimately. It's me. You know I was born in Lagos. I was actually born in the slums. Nearly 75% of Lagos is slums. I grew up down by the Makoko, the floating slum. It's part of the estuary. Thousands upon thousands of poor folk live on shanty houseboats or stick houses on the water. If you want to go anywhere, you have to go by rowboat. Some people call it Lagos' version of Venice. Those people are dreaming, in reality, the neighbourhood is one seething, raw sewage canal. The entire area stinks and oozes with decomposing garbage. The poorer residents defecate in the open. Those who are one rung higher up on the ladder use 'pit toilets' which discharge into the open canals, where many bathe. Life expectancy is low.

"My father worked the city dump. He followed the garbage truck around as it dropped its treasures. He was proud of what he did. It was an honest living.

"When I was twelve, I was begging on the streets of Lagos and was approached by a wealthy Lebanese businessman. The businessman gave me money. He came back again the next day and gave me more money. He asked me if I had eaten. I told him I hadn't, so he took me to a hole in the wall selling shawarma. He was from Beirut, but he had an office in Lagos. And he had an apartment. One day, he asked me if I wanted to see his apartment. He picked me up off the street in a Mercedes and drove me to an underground garage so no one could see him bringing someone like me into the building. It was a high rise building with a view of the floating slums. I could see our neighbourhood from his window…"

"Weren't you afraid?"

"I was overjoyed. He suggested I take a shower. I did. He had fresh clothes for me. He said that he wanted to take care of me and that I should give up begging. It was a no brainer…"

"Did he come on to you?"

"Not at the start. He taught me French and got me into a private school down on the Lekki Peninsula. He taught me how to behave. He even taught me how to walk and carry myself. He did the Pygmalion thing with me. He groomed me And got me just the way he wanted…and then he touched me. I finished high school and he got me a spot in the American University in Beirut. After I graduated from university, I returned to Lagos and he pulled strings to get me hired by Pan Am."

"Do you still see him?"

"He was killed in Beirut. Shot. No one knew who did it."

Bobby was quiet for a long time.

"I owe him everything…"

4

An Airplane Has a Certain Smell, *usually*

Our next flight to Jeddah departed just before noon, the following day. The heat was debilitating as our crew walked across the tarmac and even worse as we scurried up the moveable stairs and entered the aircraft at L2.

As before, we were overwhelmed by the steamy stench. Urine and heat just don't go down so very well. None of us first-timers had been prepared for the pungently human smells, the sour reek of a piss-ridden Boeing 747, or what a gagging stench would be created by 120-degree heat beating down all day long on what had become a gigantic flying toilet.

I should just mention that we were based in Kano for *five* weeks. And let me ask you this: Have you ever boarded an aircraft that had to make a quick turnaround, and the cleaners hadn't had enough time to thoroughly clean the aircraft? Perhaps there were still used Kleenex tissues, candy wrappers, and swizzle sticks in the seat pockets? The odd bulging barf bag? Coffee stains in the galley? Shock of shocks, no mouthwash in the lavatory?

Out of Kano, Pan Am moved between 500 and 1500 hajjis per day, for five weeks. Keep the airplane in the sky. Keep transporting. Take them up. Drop them off. Hurry, hurry.

And the airplane was not cleaned *ever* in that five-week period.

Back in Training School everything had been clinically neat and tidy. We had to be perfectly groomed and magnificently manicured and immaculately coifed. And everybody was always smiling. The instructors were smiling. The faces in all the brochures were smiling. In the emergency section of our Flight Attendant Manual, the people lost at sea in the life rafts were smiling.

Even the sharks were smiling.

I headed to the rear of the plane to my jump seat at L5. Then I consulted my watch. We wouldn't be back to our layover hotel till after midnight. With this in mind, the first officer had sneaked one lonely bottle of Star lager onboard and secreted it in the fridge of the upper-deck galley. When we came back later tonight, the bar at the hotel might be closed. This, plus, the beer served back at the bar was a bit warm by American standards, so he was really looking forward to a properly chilled adult beverage upon our return.

Soon the religious pilgrims began to board, and boarding bush people who lived in mud huts and had never set foot inside an aircraft was a bit like herding cats. Many hajjis had never climbed a set of stairs two stories high. How many mud huts have stairs? Our passengers were everywhere, exploring, pushing and shoving each other for a seat. One middle-aged pilgrim took us a while to corral. He kept extending an index finger, long and bony like the creature in the movie *E.T.* and he touched everything he could: the seats, the windows, the galley, the doorknobs to the toilets, the air vents, the bulkheads…everything. Then he put his index finger up to his nose to smell it.

Eventually, we got all the hajjis seated, seatbelts fastened, doors closed, armed, cross-checked, and we taxied down to the end of the runway. And are you ready for this? On this particular day, it took four hours to board. *Four* hours! Now we wouldn't be getting back to our layover hotel until the middle of the night.

I looked out my window and watched a Nigeria Airways DC-10 land. Finally, we were cleared for take-off. I always found take-off to be thrilling, something about the thrust and power and noise—and the ensuing destination. The nose lifted, we sprang into the air, and just like last time, the bodily fluids slowly swept aft-wards towards my jump seat. Quickly, I rolled up my trouser cuffs and lifted up my legs so my shoes wouldn't get soaked.

And the hajjis began to chant. Were they praying? It was a well-known fact that if a hajji died on the way to Mecca, they would go straight to heaven. Surely not where I was going to go if the plane went down.

I held my legs up in the air as we climbed. I sensed amused eyes staring at me and looked up to see the African passengers in my section holding their feet up in the air, imitating me. It made me laugh, and my laughter made them laugh. We laughed together long and hard, but then I suddenly stopped, and do you know why? Because that's when I realized these charmingly naïve folk from the bush of Central Africa were holding their feet up in the air, because they thought that would help the plane to fly.

We had two mops in the aft section of the plane, and once we reached our cruising altitude, Bella and I would try to mop up as much of the urine as we could. Little good it did, though, no sooner had we mopped it up, then we would find someone peeing on a bulkhead. We had an interpreter onboard, and we politely asked him to mention that it would be a great help if the passengers could attempt to use the facilities, such as they were: The toilet lids and seats had been removed from all the lavatories, and there was just a hole for them to use. We were thrilled when we finally had some success and even had a queue to use the toilets—until we realized our passengers were opening the toilet door and just peeing on the walls in there.

For our own personal use, we kept one lavatory locked on the upper deck. It was the cleanest, tidiest, most fragrantly appealing toilet you would ever hope to find on an aircraft. Even Queen Elizabeth would have been impressed, and this from a woman who takes her own toilet seat with her when she flies.

I was slowly adjusting to the overpowering stench in the aircraft. Having said that, on account of the uric acid, the entire 747 would have to be refitted once the hajj was over and that cost had been included in the details of the contract. A first officer told me that when we ferried the 747s in, the cargo hold was loaded with "requested" items used to warm the hearts of the local government, airport and customs officials. Among the items were hundreds of cases of Johnny Walker Red.

The hajjis were always getting trapped in the lavatories, so when one of them went to use the facilities, we always kept one eye on the clock. I chose to find the cultural differences charming rather than off-putting.

On one occasion, a rather young woman went into the lavatory and was in there for a long time. I told Bella and she went to check on the woman. Bella found the woman simply looking in the mirror. Mirrors were a scarce commodity in the Nigerian bush.

On another occasion, a different young lady, a *petite* young lady, was in the lavatory for an awful long time. Once again, I told Bella.

"*You* go check on her," Bella said. "I'm too busy now."

"You're not doing anything. You're sitting on your jump seat."

"*You* go check."

"But isn't it better if a woman goes check."

"*You* go check."

Often, our hajjis would close the door behind them and not be able to get out because they didn't know how to open the door from the inside. The young woman had somehow locked the door, so I used my nifty Pan Am pen and quietly slid the lock open from the outside. I knocked. Nothing. I heard water running, so I discreetly opened the door a crack. Much to my horror, the petite young woman had somehow managed to get up on the sink and she was squatting on it, using it like a bidet, wishing to arrive in Mecca "cleansed," as was custom.

That wasn't in the Flight Attendant manual!

I enjoyed working the aft section of the airplane in spite of the fact that on take-off, gravity brought us all sorts of presents. The aft section of the airplane was rewarding because it was the only place in a 747 where the flight attendant jump seats faced forward. If you faced forward, you could look through the whole airplane and watch a profoundly refreshing world at work.

But there were dangers we had to watch for, as well.

Flight #163, a Saudi Arabian Airlines L-1011, had gone down en-route to Mecca because hajjis had been allowed to carry flammable liquids and butane stoves on the plane in their carry-on luggage. "Carry-on" was a misnomer, as the hajjis brought on great big sacks of everything they would need to survive the lengthy sojourn, including food and the stoves to cook it on. Hard to imagine, but at the time, various Middle-Eastern carriers actually allowed hajjis to fire up their stoves inside the cabin. Some lit the stoves if they got cold. Others lit the stoves to make hot tea on the long flight.

In this case, a fire had started in the aft cargo hold C-3 and burnt its way up into the aft passenger cabin. Flight attendants vigorously fought the fire as the captain tried to get the aircraft on the ground.

The captain managed an emergency landing as now thick, choking smoke swept through the aircraft. The plane should have stopped immediately on the runway, but the captain wasted precious minutes taxing the aircraft off the active runway for nearly 2 minutes and 40 seconds. Why didn't he stop, evacuate the passengers and let emergency crews fight the fire? King Khalid's 747 was taxing onto the runway, and it was rumoured that if the King's 747 was rolling, *all* movement at the airport must clear the way, then stop out of deference. Did ill-fated Flight #163 waste valuable time exiting the active runway so the King could take off? Was the on-time King's departure more important than the evacuation of a burning plane?

No one should have died in this incident, but in lieu of the command to evacuate, the pilgrims panicked and they piled up, screaming, at the only door which to them resembled a door— the cockpit door, and everyone died a fiery death, poisoned by fumes, one on top of the other, clawing at a door that wasn't an exit.

In total, all 301 onboard died: 287 passengers and 14 crew

members

Following the accident, Lockheed did away with all the combustible insulation from above the rear cargo area and reinforced it with high-strength glass laminate. Saudi Arabia Airlines revised their emergency procedures and made changes to evacuation protocol. They also sealed off all C-3 baggage compartments.

As I write this, I find it difficult to believe that protocol would be so strict in a country that it would allow people to perish. Then I remembered the 15 school girls in Mecca. This from the BBC: "Saudi Arabia's religious police stopped schoolgirls from leaving a blazing building because they were not wearing correct Islamic dress, according to Saudi newspapers.

"In a rare criticism of the kingdom's powerful 'mutaween police,' the Saudi media has accused them of hindering attempts to save 15 girls who died in the fire.

"About 800 pupils were inside the school in the holy city of Mecca when the tragedy occurred.

"According to the *al-Eqtisadiah Daily*, firemen confronted police after they tried to keep the girls inside because they were not wearing the headscarves and *abayas* (black robes) required by the kingdom's strict interpretation of Islam.

"One witness said he saw three policemen beating young girls to prevent them from leaving the school because they were not wearing the *abaya*.

"The *Saudi Gazette* quoted witnesses as saying that the police—known as the Commission for the Promotion of Virtue and Prevention of Vice—had stopped men who tried to help the girls and warned 'it is sinful to approach them'."

* * *

With building fires inside an aircraft in mind, we had to be vigilant and keep our eyes open during our hajj flights. Anything could happen at any time. But despite the potential dangers, and the arresting aromas, it was fun to be with these people from a far-off land and try to talk with them in Hausa.

And when language barriers got in the way, thank goodness we had the comforting luxury of being able to fall back on those Training School smiles.

* * *

As the plane droned on, my mind drifted back to a couple of hours earlier when our passengers had boarded. The hajjis were barefooted (on a urine soaked carpet!). Each hajji brought one carry-on bag with them. The men were dressed in all white and carried their carry-on bag onto the airplane the way you and I carry a bag onboard, in their hand. The female pilgrims were also barefooted but wore colorful, sari-like wraparounds. They, too, carried just one bag onboard, but they boarded the aircraft—balancing their carry-on luggage on their heads. The women's clothes had to adhere to strict rules and consist of nothing "attractive or resemble the clothes of men, or be tight fitting or showing the dimension of their limbs, or transparent and not conceal what was underneath, or too short, not covering the legs or hands, but instead should be abundant, thick and wide."

The clothes of the hajji, the *Ihram*, are meant to reflect "the equality of all pilgrims, with no difference between a prince and a pauper." While wearing the Ihram, a "pilgrim may not shave, clip his or her nails, wear perfume, swear or quarrel, have sexual relations, uproot or damage plants, kill or harm wild animals, cover the head (for men) or the face and hands (for women), marry, wear shoes over the ankles, or carry weapons."

I also noticed the men sat in the forward half of the aircraft and all the women sat in the back half. "Hey, Bella," I yelled over to my peppery colleague. "What's with the seating arrangement, male chauvinism?"

"Male chauvinism?" Bella mocked, getting a lot out of the words. "The men think that if the plane crashes the front end will hit the ground first and they want to protect the women sitting behind."

As we continued our flight to Saudi Arabia, I looked out

at all the bobbing heads in the aircraft, and it slowly dawned on me that we had a curious amount of passengers onboard. At the time, a Boeing 747 seated around 365 passengers, depending on the configuration, but Pan Am opted to remove the Boeing 747 seats and replace them with 520 zero-legroom, Boeing 707 seats. So we had one hell of a circus onboard. It was comparable to transporting a small town, and everything that happens in a small town happens on an airplane.

Everything.

We had numerous African gray parrots traveling with us, as well. Normally this was against regulations (flocks of screeching, shitting, feathered caged creatures in the cabin), but for the hajj, apparently almost anything went. The parrots spent most of the flight chirping happily away and peeping at us as we went around the cabin mopping. The African gray was worth quite a few riyals in Mecca, and the pilgrims could trade or sell them to help pay for their trip, or buy Zamzam water (holy water from a well in Mecca) to take back home with them, so we looked the other way when our Mecca-bound passengers brought about twenty of the little feathered critters onboard.

Once, playing the clown (as oft was my wont), I took one of the parrots out of its cage and walked down the aisle with him on my shoulder. It brought down the hajji house. Imagine that happening on a New York–London?

Every so often, a young female pilgrim would come right up to me, almost touching, and put her nose very nearly against mine. The young lady would stare and stare, then giggle and run off. After this happened a number of times, I turned to Bella with a questioning look.

"How in hell's name should I know? Do I look like the bloody answer lady?"

But this kept going on, and I kept asking Bella. Finally she had a brief lapse into decency.

"It's your blue eyes, laddie. They've never seen blue eyes before. Now will ye bugger off and leave us alone."

Something in the cabin in front of me breached my

33

attention. A golden, viscous liquid was dripping down from one of the overhead compartments. Oil? I quickly rose to investigate. I watched, gobsmacked, as the liquid dripped onto the white robe of one of the male passengers. The passenger stuck his finger in the liquid, smelled it, then licked it. He looked up at the curious liquid seeping out of the overhead compartment. Not fazed, he plucked his bag out from under the seat in front of him, reached in, took out a loaf of bread and held it up to catch the drip. It was honey, and it never dawned on him that someone had placed it up there and it had somehow spilled. To him, it was just another Pan Am perk that came with the whole journey of going to Mecca.

Adorable.

Later, I was peering out the window, Africa was passing by slowly below, and I was basking in the glow of adventure when suddenly, ba-Boom! the plane hit some clear-air turbulence and shuddered the way a dog does when it's shaking off water.

The "Fasten Seatbelt" announcement was made in English, then in Hausa. Neither language did any good though. None of the pilgrims knew what a seatbelt was.

I unbuckled my shoulder harness and struggled up from my jump seat. Turbulence comes in many varieties, and today it came in waves—north shore waves. I remember spending an inordinate amount of time trying to fasten seatbelts on passengers who didn't understand how they worked. As I madly fastened belts, I saw one loving husband, an older man with snowy-white hair, make his way to the aft section of the aircraft. He was worried about his little wife. With great curiosity, he watched me fasten the seatbelts for a moment, then went to help his Mrs., but the mechanics of it all were just too much for him.

Finally, not out of frustration but out of ingenuity, he solved the problem—he simply tied the belt in a great big knot.

As I returned to my seat, the turbulence threw me side to side, and I purposely staggered like the town drunk. The female hajjis were a good audience. They started to scream with laughter. This going to Mecca was more fun than they could have ever dreamed of, and the turbulence didn't bother them. How could it? Bless their innocent hearts, most of them didn't even know what it meant to be up in the air.

I turned my attention to my passengers once more, and they watched my every move. For fun, I looked out the window and saw out of the corner of my eye that they were now all trying to look out the window. When I stopped, they stopped. I smiled at the pilgrims, and as always they all smiled great big smiles back. These were truly special people. There was a serenity and contentedness being around them that I had never felt before. The pilgrims had no idea what made an airplane fly or what jet travel was. All they had been told was if they climbed into the "long, silver tube," they would end up in Mecca and fulfill their lifelong dream.

These hajj flights should have been a living nightmare, but it was just the opposite. Oddly enough, it turned out to be a culturally remarkable experience. The people made it so. Every moment was so different from anything I had ever experienced in my life. I remember feeling very warm inside, and I knew even then, that because of its utter uniqueness, it would be a time that I would remember and treasure for the rest of my life.

Thinking back on that particular flight, I remember we arrived safely at King Abdul Aziz International Airport, in Jeddah, late at night—with the entire airplane bathed in a symphony of snores. This mass snooze lent some credence to the age-old theory that cavemen learned to snore at night so the echoing whistles, rasps and roars emanating from their cave would keep the wild animals at bay.

When the passengers finally awoke, they stared in innocent wonder at the bright, dazzling lights of a very large airport, a world decidedly alien to their own.

The deplaning began by way of a rickety set of steps down to the tarmac, and I was in the process of giving thanks that all had gone well, when I noticed one small problem (actually I should say one large problem). As the pilgrims exited the aircraft, the plane got lighter, and as the plane got lighter, it slowly started to rise on its *oleos* (an "oleo" strut is an air–oil hydraulic shock absorber used on the landing gear of most large aircraft). More and more pilgrims disembarked and the plane seemed to levitate.

The first step out of the airplane to the stairs below was becoming a lulu—but nobody realized it.

Bella and I were too busy saying goodbye to all our new found friends to notice that by the time most of the passengers had deplaned, it was almost a free fall to the moveable stairs. This is when the "large problem" came waddling down the aisle. She was a smiling, beaming, bowlful of Jell-O, bouncing, shaking woman. Bella and I waved our thumbs in the traditional Nigerian farewell and said "*Sannuka...Sannuka.*"

The bowlful of Jell-O screamed with laughter at our attempt to speak Hausa, took a step out the door and vanished.

"Bugger me! Where'd she go?" Bella yelled in horror.

Fearing the worst, I looked down. The bowlful of Jell-O was wedged between the moveable steps and the fuselage, legs dangling—and she was still screaming with laughter.

Bella and I sprang to the platform below and tried to exhume our large problem from her precarious position, but it was hopeless.

"Bella, go call for help over the intercom. Get every crew member you can!"

Bella dived into the aircraft, while I mollycoddled the woman and laughed with her to keep her calm. Within moments, the rest of the flight crew were helping us tug the cheery woman out of her dangerous predicament. And I don't know how to say this sensitively, but it was those bowlful of Jell-O attributes that had saved her life and had kept her from falling to the tarmac below.

Now, with the entire crew waving thumbs at her, the woman flashed us a smile as wide as Africa itself, and bounced, jiggled and giggled down the moveable stairs.

"Quick thinkin', Breakfield," Bella admitted. "I take back what I said about wantin' to fly with somebody more senior. Yar not a tosser. Yar alright, bonnie lad!"

After this short but distinctly unnerving excursion into airline hell, we were eager to turn the aircraft around and head back to Kano, but there was a problem: Customs had found one lonely, very cold bottle of Star lager in the upstairs galley and they went ballistic. Alcohol in the Kingdom was strictly forbidden. Indeed, the smuggling of alcohol is punishable by death. If you get a sympathetic judge, you might only get the 500 lashes. Our captain was summoned and we were threatened with fines and being detained. We all felt this was way OTT and uncalled for.

But then again, this from a country that forced schoolgirls back inside flaming buildings.

Much to the first officer's horror, the Star lager was seized and we were allowed to start up the engines. We "turned the aircraft around" and ferried the empty plane five hours back to Kano. And it was good to be back at home base, and hit the sack. Still, having said that, I couldn't wait for my next trip. And I felt that I was ready for anything and that nothing could possibly surprise me the next time around.

But it did.

A few weeks later, I was waiting for the pilgrims to board. They were all down on the tarmac, standing in the shade formed by the aircraft's wing. They had been waiting a long time and some would have to leave the queue to go to a nearby grassy strip to defecate.

Then I saw him.

I observed from the top of the moveable steps at L5, a frail elderly man. He may have been frail, but he was not about to be pushed around or left behind. This gentleman was very eager to get to Mecca and had been saving and looking forward to the journey his entire life. There was never any security or screening, so when he arrived at the airport, he simply walked out of the terminal, crossed the tarmac and found all the other younger pilgrims already standing in the shade of the 747's wing trying to keep out of the scorching heat. While his youthful colleagues patiently waited for the signal to climb the steps, I watched the elderly man sneak, beg and con his way to the front of the queue.

When it was finally time to board, the elderly pilgrim was the first one up the steps and he climbed with spiritually motivated vigor and entered the aircraft at L2 the way your doctor ebulliently enters the examining room. Obsessed now, the little old man marched all the way through the "long, silver tube" until he came to the rear of the aircraft where I was stationed. Here he stopped, gave me a *Home Alone* look, then peered out the aft door and saw the set of steps leading back down to the tarmac.

I watched in astonishment as the little man regarded the ground below, then euphorically descended the steps and overcome with the delirious frisson of excitement, knelt upon the tarmac and kissed the earth.

He thought he had arrived in Mecca.

5

Bat Strikes

Deep into our hajj flights, we were ferrying the empty aircraft back to Kano. It was the middle of the night. All the other cabin attendants were in the upper deck, sleeping.

But I wasn't.

I was sitting at L4, reading about Pan Am's founder, Juan Terry Trippe. For those of you who have never had the chance to sit in a seemingly empty 747, with ALL THE LIGHTS turned off except your one lonely reading light, let me tell you it is eerie! I was absorbed in my book, then I looked up into a black hole of nothingness. Dark aft, dark forward. I looked out my window. Dark down there, as well. The Dark Continent. Super eerie. I felt as if I were in a ghost ship. The Marie Celeste. I heard a dull thud next to my seat. I strained my neck. Sitting there next to my head was a rather impressive specimen of a praying mantis. They're big, you know. I rose and slipped over to the aft galley and rooted around until I found a large paper tub. Then I captured the gentle beast and took it upstairs to where the rest of the cabin crew were sleeping. I placed the tub upside down on the galley where everyone would be able to see it when they awoke. And I wrote in large, bold letters DO NOT TURN OVER!

Just before we began our descent in to Kano, I heard a disembodied scream come from the upstairs galley, suspiciously male.

On final approach, we had to dodge thunderstorms, then just before touching down, we had "bat strikes," no, not bird strikes—bats. The captain said that our radar might have upset the bats' radar, causing them to collide with our aircraft. That, plus bats feed on insects and swarms of insects were often attracted to the runway lights (when they were operational).

The captain mentioned that the next time we came in at night, he would turn off the radar.

After we landed, blocked and shut down the engines, some of us did a walk around with the captain and flight engineer while we were waiting for the crew bus. Using a flashlight, we could easily make out where the bats had hit.

No damage to the aircraft.

Full damage to the bats. SPLAT. We could actually make out little fossil-like bat outlines.

6

The Lebanese Club

The following evening we heard about the Lebanese Club. It was private, but invitations had been extended to all Pan Am employees.

Bella, Bobby and I took a taxi over there. The ride was through a black vastness that is much of Kano's streets at night. Can't put too much demand on the national grid when there are no streets lights. We had a near miss at one street intersection as the offending vehicle coming at us from the right hadn't bothered to switch on its headlights. Or perhaps they simply didn't work. It gave all of us quite a fright, what with it being a lorry fully loaded with cattle.

We arrived about nine and were refused entry. We showed our Pan Am IDs and magically we were rock stars. We were offered profuse apologies and warmly escorted to a darkened outdoor terrace surrounded by leafy trees and paved with orange tiles. I remember it being extremely hot and sticky humid. There was a DJ playing music, mostly American and English. The place was sardine-city. Nary a seat to be had. I spied a few other flight crews there. As I've mentioned, it was always easy to spot a flight crew. Do I need to explain this? There was a rather large scrum of what appeared to be rich Lebanese men, smoking. Or average Lebanese men who were trying to appear rich, smoking. They spent much of the evening eyeing the flight crews.

We ordered a bottle of Lebanese wine. I danced with Bella. Then Bella danced with Bobby. Then I danced with Bella again. Bella was dressed in her usual "show as much skin as possible attire." And there was something erotic about it all. The heat. The far-corner-of-the-world exoticness. Africa. The sweat. Perhaps, just a little, available alcohol in a part of the world where it was for the most part forbidden.

Late in the evening, a Canadian stewardess who flew with Martinair approached me and asked me if I wanted to dance. Was I ever the lucky one, this just didn't happen. I can't recall the young lass' name, but I do recall that she was short and dark and smoldering. We danced a few fast dances. And we sweated. And we drank red wine. And we sweated. We danced a slow dance and the air became sultry and heady. Somewhere around midnight, when I was just about to run out of sweat, she said: "Let's get out of here."

I said: "Where?"

She said: "The Star Wars Bar at the Central Hotel."

I said: "The what?"

She said: "The Star Wars Bar. That's what everyone calls it. Let's go."

I think it's safe to say that most of you reading this don't have Kano, Nigeria, on your Bucket List…therefore not the "Star Wars Bar" either, but if you do make it over to Kano, you just gotta go. It's located in the aforementioned Central Hotel. The hotel was a dump, when I was there, but the bar was out of this world. Although, having said that, possibly a bit what a migraine would look like if it could be visualized. And, no, it's not like the Star Wars Bar in the movie, no space aliens playing the clarinet with their noses.

Not yet anyway.

As we entered, we heard music pounding out. Miss Martinair noted: "Jùjú music. This style of music is common in the south of the country, not so much up here."

We looked around. Marble floor. A large golden urn in the middle of the marble floor. Subdued lighting, with miniature spots aiming at nothing in particular. And the place was mobbed. A few too many bar girls. Bottle caps everywhere on the floor. We found a cushy sofa in a corner, sat down and thought we would disappear in its depths. Everyone was watching us, so we watched everyone back. Certainly a Star Wars mix in here. Business types, playboy types, hooker types, rogue types, Nigerian and Lebanese. Lots of men, not so many women, other than the bar girls. All the men seemed to be fascinated by Miss Martinair's skirt. The shortness of it. Perhaps the toned, tanned legs. The hajj is a great place to get a tan as you are always falling asleep by the pool.

Perhaps not the best place to be scantily dressed.

A bar girl approached and we ordered some wine. We were informed that the bar did not serve alcohol.

"Not even beer and wine?"

"No alcohol."

I looked over at Miss Martinair. "Let's bolt!" she said.

"Where?"

"Let's go to a bush bar…"

Oh, oh, I was thinking. Remember me telling you about these? Those suspect establishments down a dark alley where it was advisable not to go during the day?

Miss Martinair wanted to go at night.

"You sure about this?" I said, perhaps just a bit tentatively. "There's organ trafficking here in the north, you know, and I'm rather fond of the ones I've got."

Miss Martinair said nothing, just looked back at me. For some reason with the same look on her face that Faye Dunaway gave Steve McQueen in *The Thomas Crown Affair*, when they were playing chess.

Your move.

I prattled on, trying to present my case: "Plus there's the sale of human body parts for black magic rituals. Did you know they go after the eyes and genitals? We will be kidnapped, dismembered and what's left of us will be dumped in a dried-up well."

"Can't be that bad…"

"Can't be that bad! How can having your privates lopped off and getting dumped in a rat-infested, dried-up well, not be bad?"

Miss Martinair laughed. "Where's your sense of adventure?" This said with a twinkle in her eye. A *sensuous* twinkle in her eye.

Your move.

I studied Miss M for a moment, she had curious subtext going, but I couldn't get past the sex appeal. I wasn't going to risk being emasculated just for a shot at getting laid, was I?

"Taxi!" I yelled as we exited the Central Hotel and walked the usual gauntlet of utterly creepy men who seem to enjoy milling about out front of Nigerian hotels. A taxi materialized out of nowhere. The cab was an old Mercedes with at least a quarter-million miles on it. A diesel, by the smell of it. We jumped in. The taxi was really hot and it stank of a quarter-million miles of body odor.

"Bush bar," Miss Martinair told the driver.

The *driver* eyed us in the mirror. "No go night," he said. "No go night."

"Bush bar," she said firmly.

And our cabbie reluctantly let out the clutch.

We rattled along through darkened, filthy streets filled with litter. We saw a few people asleep out in front of shacks. Or were they corpses?

There were no street lights here, as well, and it was creepy. It was very strange to motor down streets on the outskirts of a major city and not see street lights. Nor lights from houses or businesses. *Just great*, we were going to a Nigerian bush bar, never to be seen again. Every so often, the taxi's headlights would cut a swath through the darkness and we would see a dead animal lying in the road. Usually I'm a bit of a chatterbox, but I couldn't seem to make even a peep. What was I supposed to say?

And then Miss Martinair surprised me by speaking Hausa: "*Canza zuciya...zuwa prin din.*"

"*Lafiya!*" the cabbie responded.

"You speak Hausa?"

"Just a little."

"What else do you know how to say in Hausa?"

"My hovercraft is full of eels."

"Really?"

"No," Miss M teased. When she teased she slid very close and brushed up against me.

44

Well, dear reader, we turned down a few more absolutely pitch-black streets, drove through a no-man's land and popped out right in front of my hotel!

"This is my hotel! How'd you know where Pan Am was staying?"

"We're staying in the same hotel. Bet you never noticed."

"I did, it's just the Lebanese *vino* taking command of my brain." I must have looked a bit relieved that we didn't get eviscerated at a bush bar with manky toilets.

"You didn't really think I'd drag you off to a bush bar, did you?"

"What did you say to the cabbie?"

"I said, I changed my mind, take us to the Prince Hotel."

I leaned forward, paid the driver, gave him a "happy to still be alive" tip and we jumped out of the taxi. Miss Martinair put her arm through mine as we walked past the usual suspects guarding the entrance to our hotel. I think they were all high on alco-pops.

We decided on a nightcap, and went into the bar. I needed a stiff one. I'm talking about a drink. Franky was working. He looked at me, then at Miss M. She greeted Franky in Hausa: "*Sannu ya ya kuke.*"

"Teach me that," I said.

"*SANNU–YA–YA–KUKE.*"

I repeated: "*Sannu ya ya kuke.*"

And Franky didn't giggle, he absolutely roared.

Miss Martinair ordered a greyhound, and I ordered a Star. We lapped at our drinks. Miss M told me she had been flying for ten years and this was her seventh hajj. Thus the smattering of Hausa. I found this really cool.

"What's the attraction?" I asked.

"The attraction?"

"To keep coming back and do the hajj?"

"The people. And the heat. It can never be too hot for me."

I asked her how a Canadian got a job with Martinair.

I thought she would say that her mother or father was

Dutch, but she didn't, just that she had been living in Amsterdam and working in a coffee shop and had learned Dutch.

"So you like languages?"

"My raison d'être."

Me, too.

Miss Martinair now studied me. "Let's go back to your room," she eventually said. "I'm feeling the wine and lack of sleep." She went on to say that her roommate was having the hajj equivalent of Delhi Belly and her room was a no-go zone.

But wait! What if San-Juan Juan was back in our room getting jacked on Nigerian ditch weed? Then I remembered that he said he was flying out earlier that evening.

But wait! I knew very little about this young lady.

But wait! Who cares!

Alright, I want you to think about the most erotic, kinky one-night stand that you've ever had. You know, the one where two sweaty bodies threw off shimmering heat and orgasm came in wave after wave. Did you think about it? Well, it wasn't like that for us. Miss Martinair asked if she could use the toilet to freshen up. She went in. Was gone a bit long, I thought. I guess she was in there doing whatever it is that women do when they say they just need to freshen up first. Was she having a shower? Looking through the bathroom cabinet? Slipping into something more comfortable, like nothing? Finally, she came out. She didn't look refreshed, rather extremely pissed off.

"Are you out of your fucking mind!" she yelled, and blew out the door.

What was that all about? My mind raced, but had trouble getting through the alcohol and the down-line fatigue. Eventually, I went into the bathroom. What made her act that way? I was confused and just a little saddened. I went back in the bedroom and crawled up on my bed and fell asleep without evening turning the lights off.

And it wasn't until the next morning that I figured it out. Not until I pulled back the shower curtain and saw a mound of what appeared to be deep green oregano hidden in the bathtub.

7

Disease, Hunger, and the Basque Country

Disease.

During our African flights, when we weren't worried about passenger safety, we were all concerned about contracting some hideously tropical condition: "filariasis," for example. You may not know the name, but the results most certainly. With filariasis, a parasitic worm infestation is transmitted through the bite of a mosquito. Once inside the host (you and me), the worms hang out in the lymph nodes. Blockage of these nodes may cause grotesque enlargement of the legs, and get ready for this, even the scrotum, vulva, breast and penis (you've possibly already received this latter tidbit as email spam).

Indeed, you may not know the name, but the result—elephantiasis—sent shivers through us all. If this wasn't sincerely frightening enough, many other diseases were positively lying in wait: yellow fever, typhoid, dengue, malaria, schistosomiasis, Chikungunya fever, trypanosomiasis (African Sleeping Sickness) and River Blindness, to offer but a choice few.

For those of you hungering for knowledge, River Blindness is transmitted by blackflies that breed near fast-flowing rivers. When the flies bite people they deposit microscopic larvae which mature under the skin and produce thousands of micro-worms. Am I holding your attention here, or are you drifting off? The worms cause woeful itching and cavernous skin lesions. Left untreated, they ravage the eye, scar its delicate subcutaneous tissue and mercilessly blind their victims. In Africa, 126 million people are at risk.

With these maladies in mind, we gladly suffered numerous inoculations, devoured malaria pills and, every time we had the chance, popped open a bottle of nasal-shattering Dettol and clinically swabbed down anything we came in contact with. Big 500ml bottles of Dettol were located all over the plane, so we could sluice the cabin walls and windows next to where we sat and free the area of an absolute hit parade of dangerously nasty germs, rank smells and parrot poop from those African greys brought onboard each trip. The parrots were brought onboard in cages, but every once in a while one managed to make a bid for freedom. A few flight attendants pursuing a parrot through a packed 747 was quite good sport and our passengers always found it quite amusing. When it was time for take-off or landing, we would stow six or more cages in each of the lavatories and seal them off from the outside. The parrots didn't seem to mind this arrangement.

There were no movies or entertainment channels on these flights, and we didn't do a dinner service or breakfast service or drinks. Often, we didn't even push a trolley through the aisles, just handed out a box lunch and bottles of water. And when it was time to pick up—against Pan Am protocol—we toted large garbage bag through the aisle. And we wore, not our traditional uniforms, rather "summer" uniforms to deal with the heat: short-sleeved shirts or blouses, no ties, no jackets.

We didn't do emergency demonstrations. If the hajjis couldn't deal with a door knob, how would they deal with an oxygen mask dropping down? Can you imagine them understanding the announcement: "In case there is a change in cabin pressure, yellow oxygen masks will deploy from the ceiling compartment located above your head…"

Perhaps a more accurate announcement should have been: "In case there's a tremendous drafty whoosh in the cabin caused by life-threatening loss of air, a rubber jungle will drop right in your face and scare the living shit out of you…"

Anyway, phraseology aside, none of us wanted to think about any scenario like this. Are you getting the picture here? No oxygen mask demo. No life vest demo. No pointing out the exits. God help us if the plane went down.

The disinfectant was part of our armory, but it wasn't our first line of defense. Our first line of defense was the "Space Blanket." Space Blankets were yellow, quilt-like, and space-age composite on one side and sheep-age woolly on the other. We covered our jump seats with them, then, whenever we had a break, sat right in the middle and tried not to touch anything that hadn't been disinfected. These unusual precautions gave us a little island of protection in the middle of a seething ocean of nameless muck.

Taking no prisoners, I inundated the bulkhead around my seat with more Dettol, and as the industrial-strength aroma swirled around me, I cast my mind back to the curious series of events that now had me cocooned in a Space Blanket, disinfecting a 747, flying 37,000 feet above a swiftly-flowing African river.

I had been living in France's Basque Country, in a seaside resort just south of Biarritz called St. Jean-de-Luz. The Basque Country had always intrigued me, so I'd moved there. I had always been fascinated with languages, so I'd spent a winter in Kitzbühel, Austria, learning German, another couple months in the Canary Islands studying Spanish, and now here I was in the Basque Country hoping to improve my French. When I was younger and wanted to visit a far-off land, I often just packed up and moved. That was my approach to travel. It never crossed my mind to be a tourist and just visit. Finding some sort of job and living there was the only way to really get to know the people and get a grasp of the language.

Besides, I didn't have enough money to be a tourist.

It seemed all my friends knew what they wanted to do with their lives, but not me, I just wanted adventure, languages, and I wanted to see the world.

And money was no object—because I had no money.

I've always been a bit of a romantic, so I also hoped that answers to many questions I had would fall from the heavens. (A bird shit on me in France once, and I took that as a bad start, until I later found out the French consider it to be a good omen.)

The Basque Country could not have been more idyllic, or more seductive, but within a few months of living there, I was running out of money, and other than some work down at the boatyard, the glamorous menial work was being elusive. So here I was getting the language and the adventure—starving.

* * *

I paid a visit to the library in the centre of the picturesque seaside town and found a lonely copy of the *International Herald Tribune*. I turned to the Sports Section. I hoped by reading the Sports, my mind would be taken off the pack of hunger-emboldened wolves that had taken up residence just outside my timbered front door.

The first thing I read was how some pro athletes were complaining because they were only making ten million over three years, with incentives (and free prescription painkillers).

It started to rain, so I stalled. Better to be depressed at a French library where the mood was institutionally somber, I figured, than at home where my mind could turn to thoughts such as food or paying next month's rent.

Eventually I went from Sports to the hard stuff, Business and the Obituaries. I saved the Classifieds till after the Obituaries because they would put me in the right mood to look for a job.

I don't know why I was reading the Want Ads because there was never a job description that remotely fit me anyway. Every ad wanted some super-qualified, ambitiously experienced superhuman. Employers seemed to be looking for the kind of guy who changed his clothes in a phone booth, and that just wasn't me.

I read through the *Herald Tribune* Want Ads, and something else caught my attention. Made my eyes bulge, actually:

PAN AMERICAN WORLD AIRWAYS
HIRING
FLIGHT ATTENDANTS
MUST BE FLUENT IN GERMAN

WILLING TO RELOCATE

Pan Am! They had the most recognizable logo in the world next to Coca-Cola. They were the best airline in the world. The most glamorous airline in the world. The best paying airline in the world. When I came to Europe the last time, I flew Pan Am from LA to London. The back of the plane was empty, so I'd changed seats and stretched out on the four middle seats. But I wasn't alone. In the next row, was a young lady by the name of Susan Lovejoy. She was a flight attendant for Transamerica Airways, a charter airline based in Oakland, California. She'd had a few days off and she was on her way to Paris—to shop! How cool was that? We chatted all the way across the pond, and I kept her from sleeping, and I told her about how I loved languages and travelling, and when she realized I wasn't going to shut up, she told me about all the exotic places she flew to from Hawaii to Moscow to Aruba to Africa.

"We had a flight to Cape Town once, but had to divert to an airport in Angola to refuel. Problem was, the tower said we couldn't start up until we paid."

"Why didn't you just leave?"

"They placed a fire engine in front of us on the tarmac. The captain was not happy I can tell you that, but the day was saved by a flight attendant who could speak Portuguese. Probably didn't hurt that she was gorgeous."

"What'd you do?"

"We passed the hat."

"What!"

"We passed the hat. It was a 747. We had 365 passengers onboard and raised nearly $40,000. We gave out receipts once we reached our cruising altitude."

"The passengers weren't upset?"

"It was hot, we had been sitting on the ground for a few hours and it was starting to get dark. They were more than happy to chip in."

I looked at Susan Lovejoy. She had a radiance about her that comes with *joie de vivre*. I was immensely impressed.

Then she said these words: "So, if you like languages and travelling, why don't you fly for an airline?"

Susan Lovejoy and I became really good friends—and she had a wicked sense of humour—she would ring me from the far ends of the earth and wake me up in the middle of the night. The phone would wretch me from my sleep, I would answer, sleepily and hear: "I'm in Bangkok!" or "I'm in Rio!" or "I'm in Honolulu!"

Susan Lovejoy planted the proverbial seed.

But was Pan Am hiring males? I didn't remember any males on my Pan Am flight to London. I reread the ad. There was no mention that males were *verboten*, just the language requirement.

I had learned German when I'd spent that winter in Kitzbühel, in the Austrian Alps, but the German dialect spoken in the Tyrol was curiously perplexing. Once at a butcher's, I was supposed to order *Kalbs Knöchel* (calf's knuckle) for the neighbour's Alsatian, but I mistakenly asked for *Kalbs Knödel*. Everyone in the butcher's became hysterical, and I couldn't understand why. At the time I marvelled at the jolly nature of the locals. (Later I found out *Kalbs Knödel*, in the local dialect, means "calf's penis.")

I decided to apply for Pan Am even though I knew there would be tons of competition. I figured I had to do something to be different from the other applicants, so instead of sending a letter requesting an application as the advert had instructed, I decided to send them a fax. Not wildly creative, I now know, but I was living in the Dark Ages back then, and it was only 1972.

Right down the street from where I lived along the waterfront on Boulevard Thiers was a "Fax Boutique." Leave it to the French. So I faxed. And they faxed back! "In receipt of your fax. Application on the way."

Wow. Off to a great start. And about time. Things didn't always go so well for me when it came to trying to get a job. The application arrived. It said: *Fill out application and phone for preliminary telephone interview.* The number had a patently distant area code, but I didn't care. I was giddy from the wafting scent of opportunity.

There was no public pay phone in the town and cell phones were still a geek's dream on paper, so I had to go down to the local post office. I entered a narrow phone booth (thankful that I didn't have to change my clothes) and dialed.

"Personnel. Judy McFadden speaking."

"Hi, my name's Breakfield, and I'm calling long distance from…"

"Hey, you're the fellow who sent us the fax."

They knew who I was.

"That was a really refreshing way to contact us. Odd—but refreshing."

They thought it was refreshing.

"It really got our attention. The fax machine makes a heck of a racket when a fax comes in."

Wow. This Judy McFadden was beyond friendly.

Judy McFadden asked me if I spoke German. I told her I did—in German.

Judy McFadden began laughing.

"Is my German that bad?" I asked.

"No, not at all. It sounded really good. I'm laughing because I don't speak German."

"What do you speak?"

"I speak French."

Now get this: My French was not that bad. You see, I had been walking into all the shops in St. Jean-de-Luz acting as if I were going to buy something just to practice my French (and to practice buying something if I ever had any money).

"Well, why don't I tell you how good my German is—in French?"

It made her laugh again. I liked the sound of her laugh. I wanted to meet this Judy McFadden.

The one thing I could always do was talk. So I talked. And I talked. All nice expensive long-distance talk. I was feeling good that this friendly lady was so interested in what I did. It seemed as if we were on the phone for a lifetime and had known each other forever.

Finally, she told me they wanted to interview me—in person.

"In person, really? Where will this interview be?" I asked, as a dark cloud started to form over my head.

"Here, in Frankfurt. We'll send you the details."

"I'm looking forward to meeting you," I said. I thanked Judy, hung up the phone and screamed "Frankfurt!" Frankfurt was on the other bloody side of the planet as far as I was concerned. It would take me two days changing trains to get there from the Basque Country, and where would I get the money to go? I paid for my long, long-distance phone call and was shocked by the cost: nearly $100!

Now I was in trouble.

No, make that financial peril.

I was going to have to break into what remained of my emergency funds.

8

Swedish Squeals on the Train to Frankfurt

The train ride from the Basque Country to Frankfurt did not go so well for me.

On my trip through the night via Paris, I ended up in a compartment with a randy French sailor (who chain smoked) and four blond Swedish goddesses. "Modesty" must not be a word that exists in the Swedish language, for the girls, when they were getting ready for bed, stripped down to *just their panties* while they giggled and tittered and searched in slow motion through their backpacks for a T-shirt to sleep in. I couldn't get undressed because I was trapped on the top bunk with an elephantitis-sized erection. I don't know what the French sailor's story was, but he, too, was lying on his stomach.

I think the Swedish girls were disporting for us. On purpose.

When the lights were turned out, my head (and other parts of my body may I add) absolutely pounded with carnal fantasy until I fell into a hyper-sexual agitated sleep. And soon I was having aberrant, libidinous Nordic dreams.

Then it must have been just a little while later when I startled bolt upright in bed thinking one of the *Svenska flickas* had uttered my name. But alas, no. They were just four lumps under wool blankets looking cuddly and inviting. I tried desperately to fall asleep again and get back to a certain red barn in Sweden, but I couldn't get out of the Alsace.

I awoke again, about an hour later, to little breathy Swedish squeals, only to find the French sailor in bed with one of the Swedish girls, and they were doing thrillingly rapturous things to each other (things I never even knew were possible, growing up in Wisconsin).

This carnal peep-show, right in front of my face, brought a certain dimension of challenge to anything resembling sleep. It was shocking. It was disgusting. It was outrageous. Why didn't this ever happen to me?

In the morning, I ordered a miniature continental breakfast, and an extra-strength Tylenol, from a miniature man wearing a smart white jacket and a large bow tie. It looked as if a bat had grabbed him by the throat. The little man, who was pushing an ambitiously overloaded cart through the carriage, presented me with my miniature breakfast and a monstrous bill. But the little man was interesting. He seemed to speak all European languages and took uncommon pride in his little business. He was a good lesson for us all, I decided. I wrote down my observations of the miniature man on a miniature napkin he had given me, and then, before I knew it, the train was on the outskirts of an immense and impressive city and we were slowing. I saw a sign out one of the windows: "Frankfurt *West Bahnhof*." Soon after, we were pulling into Frankfurt's *Hauptbahnhof*, the main station.

The sun was breaking out from behind the clouds and the air was cool. Since I had time to kill, I took a stroll to explore this great city. Frankfurt am Main has a nice feel to it. It is generally known as "the smallest of Europe's big cities," and it is graced with the only skyscraper skyline in Germany. The skyscrapers, and more than 400 financial institutions, have given rise to nicknames such as "Mainhattan" and "Bankfurt." Frankfurt is without question the transportation hub of Europe, and it boasts the continent's second-largest airport and busiest train station. Those who contend that Frankfurt is just a wee bit dull, point out that it has all this transportation activity because what people really want to do is get out of town. But I didn't. I wanted to stay. I had a good feeling about the town, my interview, everything.

Now, catch this: Here I am absolutely beguiled with Frankfurt (and ready to spread word-of-mouth kudos to anyone and everyone I may meet in the future), when I return to the main train station and approach the information counter and some cow greets me with the same enthusiasm Meryl Streep was greeted with at the death camp in *Sophie's Choice*. I'd simply asked how far it was to the airport, and that seemed to be a punishable offense (why do they let these miserable sods remain on the front line?). I was eventually informed, under significant duress, it would take me about a half an hour to get there by bus, and it would cost twenty deutsche marks each way. I bought a return ticket and fled Frankfurt.

It seemed more practical to stay at a dirt-cheap pension out near the airport. That way I would be closer to my interview at the Sheraton Frankfurt Airport Hotel the next morning. Getting stuck on a bus somewhere in the middle of Frankfurt's rush hour the next day was not my idea of low stress. Better that I should get stuck in Frankfurt's rush hour today.

The bus left from the *Hauptbahnhof* and wended its way in some sort of bafflingly circuitous route, until I finally arrived at the airport. I stepped off the bus, looked around and suddenly a wave of panic swept over me.

It was a very modern airport, set way out and away from anything resembling a dirt-cheap pension. And the only hotel I could see was the luxurious, elegant, larcenous Sheraton Frankfurt Airport Hotel.

"How much is a room for the night," I asked the front desk clerk. "A cheap room. The cheapest you've got, actually."

The front-desk clerk was just as insufferable as the cow back at the train station. That, plus, he looked like Josef Goebbels, only shorter and with a more prominent nose. He peered condescendingly at me over his spectacles for a moment.

"Six hundred marks."

Six hundred D-marks! That was extortion. For that amount of money I could catch the shuttle bus over to the terminal, buy a ticket and fly to a country with cheaper rooms (and more courteous citizens).

"How much was the room?"

"Same as when you asked before."

"Does that include breakfast?"

He rolled his eyes and nodded.

I excused myself for a moment. Here I was about to fork over a small fortune to the poster child for bad customer service, and he was giving me attitude to boot! I sought temporary refuge in a glistening marble corner, stood behind a Romanesque pillar and counted my dwindling funds by a gushing fountain. When I returned to the front desk, I had trouble speaking.

"I'll take it," I said, in a tone barely audible.

"*Wie, bitte?*"

"Yes, that will be fine. I'll take the room." I wondered if for that price it was "fractional ownership."

Upstairs, in my way too comfortable, way too elegant, way too five-star room, I looked at the digital clock on my Blaupunkt T.V. with nothing but German channels. The digital clock said, 13:35, Wednesday. Breakfast began at 6:00am, Thursday.

And I didn't have any more money.

I took my one-and-only white shirt out of my bag. It had more wrinkles than a St. Pauli whore, with tenure. I picked up the telephone to dial Housekeeping to ask for an iron, but I realized I didn't have any money for the tip. Maybe it would have been no big deal to accept the iron but at the time I found it all a bit embarrassing. I put the phone down and was hit with a brainstorm. I lifted up my mattress and spread my shirt out on the bedsprings below. You know when you have a problem and it's recommended that you "sleep on it?" Well, that's exactly what I was going to do.

I took a shower and sat under the steamy water for an eternity. When I had finished, I felt better. Maybe things weren't so bad after all. I turned on the T.V. and watched a German romantic-comedy that was neither romantic nor humorous. I changed channels and found a food program that was set in Bavaria and it talked about all the German delicacies that are indigenous to that area.

And that's when the hunger began to set in. There's

nothing more of a catalyst to loneliness than hunger. And being in a strange city, in a strange hotel room, watching a program about German *Schnitzel* and *Kartoffelsalat*, didn't help.

I wanted my mother.

9

My First Interview, Yikes…

I was standing outside the doors to the breakfast room the next morning when they opened at 6am.

And I stayed until nearly 8.45am. I read all the morning newspapers and I sampled all the delights on offer. I drank most of their coffee and I visited the facilities twice. I even slipped a few extra croissants into a napkin to eat on the train ride back down to the Basque Country.

My nerves were over-caffeinated bare wires as I took the elevator up to the ninth floor for my interview, but I knew all the butterflies would soon fly away. I had a friend in the enemy camp. I couldn't wait to meet Judy McFadden. I had allowed myself just enough time. All I had to do was walk out of the elevator and walk right into the room.

The elevator came to a stop and I sprang out, propelled by 2¾ hours of caffeine consumption. The number of the interview room had been left for me at the front desk. I fished it out of my pocket and stood there for a moment trying to decipher which way the room was. The interview was in room 909. The little signs on the wall said 901-932 to the right and 933-960 to the left, so I scampered off to the right. When I arrived at room 909, I was shocked to see the door wide open and a maid in there hoovering. I asked the maid, in German, where Pan Am was, but she was Turkish and didn't understand my query. This mystery started to gnaw on the few nerves that hadn't short-circuited. I looked at my watch and it was almost 9am. I didn't know a lot about the airline business but common sense told me, DON'T BE LATE! I would have to go back downstairs and ask at the front desk. There's no way I would be on time now.

Then, just when I thought things could only get worse,

they suddenly got better. As I pressed the button to summon the elevator the piece of paper with the room number scribbled on it fell onto the five-star carpeting. And that's when my luck changed, you see, when I picked the piece of paper up again it no longer read 909, now it read 606.

The race was on again. The elevator I wanted, decided to go down before it wanted to come up to me. I jabbed at the elevator buttons, but the elevators were nowhere near my floor. I kept jabbing, but the elevators kept creeping farther away. (Why is it that elevators know we're in a hurry, and why is it they continually conspire against us?) I had no choice, I lunged at a nearby door and sprinted down three flights of stairs and collapsed onto the landing of the sixth floor. TICK. TICK. TICK. TICK.

And then for some reason I became very calm and started to laugh. What was I worrying about? Judy McFadden had a great sense of humour. We would spend the first part of the interview talking about old times and laughing at my folly. I knocked on the door, and after a few moments, a woman, who I thought was a dead ringer for Eva Braun, answered.

"Hi, my name's Breakfield. I'm here to see Judy McFadden. Are *you* Judy McFadden?"

Eva just raked me from top to bottom the way a carnivore does before it seizes its prey and said in a pompously heavy-German accent "*Fräulein* McFadden eeze *nicht* here. Vat did you say your name vas?"

"Breakfield."

Eva pulled out a clipboard and mashed through the type-written pages. "Don't see your name anyvere on zee list *Herr* Bruchfeld. Are you one hundred percent sure you vere inwited for an interwoo?"

"One hundred percent," I heard my voice croak, but I was thinking more like fifty-one percent, at best. How could this be? I know I had been given an interview date, but suddenly I was starting to doubt it. Perhaps they had really told me to stay away.

"I'm sorry *Herr* Bruchfeld, zere must be some mishtake.

Now if you'll excuse me…"

"But I was invited!" I said, as Eva shut the door in my face. "I'm the guy who faxed!"

I was staring at the closed door, not smiling this time, when I heard someone coming down the corridor. I turned and saw a vision of femininity strolling toward me.

"Jon?"

"Yes," I said.

"I'm Judy McFadden."

"Judy McFadden! You don't know how happy I am to see you." And I *was* happy. I was happy, because now I knew I was saved, that everything was going to be all right, and perhaps just a little, you understand, because Judy McFadden was simply the most gorgeous woman I had ever set eyes upon.

"And we're happy to see you," she said, trying to keep from laughing. I wondered why everybody I ever dealt with always seemed as if they were trying to keep from laughing.

"You're early," Judy added.

"I know, I wanted to make an impression."

"You have," she said, as her face came alive with laughter. "You're ten days early."

"Ten days!"

"Better early than late in the airline business," she said, being supportive when she could have been critical. "What language were you speaking when these arrangements were made?"

"German," I said proudly. And I was proud because I understood the Nominative, Accusative, Genitive and Dative Cases. And I understood the Imperfect, the Pluperfect, the Conditional and the Subjunctive. I understood it all. If I didn't understand the language so well I wouldn't be standing here right now.

"Well, we had you down for the seventeenth, not the seventh. Perhaps it sounds a bit similar in German."

On this, the door to the room opened and Eva, who had a mouth like the Lincoln Tunnel, bellowed from within the room, "*Ja,* similar, but not zee same. Your German, *Herr*

Bruchfeld. Your German could cost you deez job!"

On this, Judy McFadden flashed me a sexually transmitted smile and said these gut-wrenching words: "You can have your interview today, but I won't be able to do it."

"Who's going to do it?"

"She will," she said, pointing at Eva.

I peered into the room and Eva was eyeing me like a naughty child she was about to spank. "Come," she said, very head mistress. *"Mach' schnell."*

I entered, and an oppressively evil perfume slapped me twice across the face. I was dead. I had no chance with a woman who had broader shoulders than I did.

Eva picked up an ominous looking note pad, exhaled like a subway train and bleated: "Do you schmoke?"

"No, thanks."

"Zat eeze not vat I meant, I asked zee question, because you schmell of schmoke."

"I do?"

"Ja, you do. *Wery* strongly."

"Well, I still don't schmoke, I mean smoke."

"Hmm. Hmmm." She eyed me suspiciously and made a protracted entry on her pad of paper.

"So," she spat, "vee commence zee interwoo, *ja?"*

"Ja," I gulped, and we were off and running much to my terror. I felt so insecure. I'm not so very good at interviews. Sure, I'm a friendly kind of guy who smiles a lot, but I'm not very good at these things. It reminded me of when I was a kid in high school basketball. I was lousy in practice but always did well in the games, but I never got picked for the games—because I was always so lousy in practice.

I glanced over at the bed next to Eva. I was having trouble concentrating on the questions. I was afraid Eva never had anything resembling a man this close to a bed before.

Eva asked tricky questions, trying to catch me out. "So, if your boss eeze a vooman (when she said vooman, it sounded like a BMW changing gears), vould zat bother you—you being a man?"

"No, that wouldn't bother me. If she is my boss, she is the most qualified for the job. I, as a simple, humble, insignificant, numb-nuts trainee, will do whatever she asks, obediently." Perhaps those weren't my exact words, but that was the subtext.

Eva liked that response.

I looked at the bed again.

Eva droned on.

I glanced around the room. Because I hadn't slept so well the past nights, my eyes started to play tricks. I saw swastikas and Nazi banners hanging from all the walls. I shook my head. Now Eva had a moustache. I shook my head again.

"Do you mind relocating?"

"I look forward to relocating."

She kept making notes.

"Do you mind voorking Sundays?"

"Actually, I love to work on the weekends."

"Do you mind voorking in zee middle of zee night?"

"It's when I voork, I mean, work best." Shit, I was duplicating her accent again. I always did that.

"*Gut, Herr* Bruchfeld."

"Breakfield."

"Vatever. Now vee continue in *Deutsch*."

And she did. And I did. And I thought this nightmare would never end. Just when it seemed to be going the worst, something magical happened, I simply gained control of my nerves, and because I was no longer nervous, I relaxed and she saw the real me. I was in the game. It wasn't practice. And I was winning.

After copious note taking, and a little erasing on Eva's part, I knew I had won her over to my side. She really was quite sweet.

The banners and the swastikas were gone, and I felt I had a good chance at the job. She rose. I rose. She walked toward me and extended her hand. I extended mine.

"Congratulations," she said, "I vould like to congratulate you for today you have succeeded und zats why vee vould love to tell you zat you have been selected..."

My mind danced with glorious visions: *Yes? Yes? Really? Is it true? At last I have a job? Do I really get to work for Pan American World Airways? When do I start? What interesting parts of the world do I get to fly to? How much money can I make in overtime? Per diem? What do the stewardesses look like? Will I get in trouble if I call them "stewardesses"?*

"...to come back here to Frankfurt for a second interwoo."

SECOND FRIGGIN' INTERVIEW!!! I said this in my mind, but it was so loud I hoped she hadn't heard. I couldn't believe it. I didn't have enough money to run around Europe, staying and starving in the finest hotels—interwooing.

"Great!" I said, with a twitchy smile. "That's all I could hope for."

"Oh, and *Herr* Bruchfeld. One other thing. You dress nice. Zats important because vee have schtrict dress codes *mit* our airline. Do me a favour for zee next time, von't you?"

"Yes, of course, anything."

"Be sure to iron your shirt, *ja?*"

10

Training School Begins

Remember this?

"Ladies and gentlemen, we will be arriving at Miami International Airport in just a few minutes…"

The aircraft banked, and I looked out the window but couldn't see anything except dark menacing clouds.

The plane was on final approach, descending lower and lower, when it began to sway back and forth. Side to side. A motion that normally would lull a person to sleep, but not tonight. Not in this weather.

Lower we came. Still lower. Not long now. Seconds from touchdown. Suddenly a jolt. Then another. And WHOOSH! the aircraft dropped out of the sky SLAMMED the ground with a horrifying splitting sound.

Here's the rest of the story:

A bit shaken, I wobbled away from the mock-up aircraft with my other classmates, who had been posing as passengers, glad this part of Emergency Training was over.

"Did you have to scream so loudly, Ruth?" I said to one of my fellow trainees. "You didn't have to make it sound so real. It scared the hell out of me."

"Scared the hell out of you?" said a another classmate, Stan Oliver, "Scared the shit out of me."

"I wasn't trying to make it sound real. I was that scared," Ruth said, defending her emotional outburst. "That simulator made everything seem like it was actually happening."

"Well, just a couple more days of Emergency Training," I said. "Then it'll all be over. All we have to do now is swim with the sharks, inflate the life rafts and pass the final."

"Our class won't be swimming with the sharks in Biscayne Bay," Stan said. "We're doing the exercise in the pool."

"They have sharks in the pool?"

We dreaded "Emergency Week." It was the most difficult part of our four weeks of Training and if you hadn't flunked out on account of the physical, your weight, your attitude, your weight, being late, your weight, your foreign languages, your weight, breaking down and crying like a wee babe from all the stress, your weight, producing *green* scrambled eggs, your weight, you flunked out of Training School because of "Emergency."

When I first arrived at Training School I didn't know what to expect. None of us did.

We were a diverse group in my training class, from all over the world, and the vast majority were female. I reasoned that there was a good chance I would be able to throw off my weighty mantle of having zero luck with women if I worked for the airline. If a young damsel worked for Pan Am, she liked to travel and if she liked to travel, she probably liked adventure.

In my class there were two young ladies from Sweden, three from England, three from Australia, one from Denmark and one from tiny Tonga. China, Nigeria, Norway, Ireland, Switzerland, Germany, France, Finland, Malaysia, Scotland and America were also represented.

Between us we spoke over twenty languages and a whole lot of interesting dialects. We heard bizarre dialects being spoken from Nigeria, China and Malaysia, but we all concurred the strangest dialect we had ever heard in our lives (besides Glaswegian), was Ruth's Swiss-German.

I speak of Ruth often here because Ruth was a stunner in the looks department—and she reminded me of Judy McFadden. Of course everything had eventually turned out fine in Frankfurt. I somehow survived my second interview and I was hired along with over 400 others worldwide out of over 400,000 applicants. We had college degrees, were multi-lingual and were about to fly with the most prestigious airline in the world where we would have seven-to-ten-day trips, with two-to-three-day layovers, and a month's vacation a year.

I was over the moon.

Yes, everything had gone fine except finding out that Judy McFadden was married to a 747 captain with fifteen years seniority (and an attractive pension plan). But there were other fish in the sea and I was now in the airline business which would allow me to cruise the seven seas (or at least fly 37,000 feet above them).

Pan Am shipped me out to Miami and I remember feeling socially unfit and sartorially ill-dressed sitting in Pan Am First Class on my way from Frankfurt to London and then London to New York. Presidents, rock stars, royalty, movie stars, millionaires, flew Pan Am First Class, not some desperate lost soul who nicked chocolate croissants from the buffet at the Sheraton Frankfurt Airport Hotel.

I was seated in the last row of First Class, next to an elegantly dressed French cow who seemed inordinately pissed off that someone was seated next to her who wasn't filthy rich, famous and available. Just after the Fasten Seatbelt sign PINGED off, I rose and went over to the First Class purser and asked if I could move back.

She was an older, yet an exceedingly glamorous and handsome woman. And she was kind. "But you are already in the back row..."

"I mean back in economy."

"Coach?"

"Yes, please."

"But aren't you heading to Training School to become a flight attendant?"

"Yes."

"You will have to work First Class one day, you know," she said, impressing me by being clairvoyant.

"I'm hoping they will mold me."

She looked at me and I thought she was going to scold me, but she didn't, rather she whispered conspiratorially: "They will. I went in a girl and came out a woman..." And she gave me a comforting wink.

I hope I don't come out a woman is what I was thinking.

I thanked the First Class purser, turned, and did a face-plant into the chest of a rather tall First Class passenger.
It was Warren Beatty.
I wanted to crawl in a hole.
In spite of my incursion with Warren Beatty, I decided to stay in my First Class seat and observe, albeit through a fugue of smoke being emitted by the *vache* nightmare sitting *à côté de moi*.

The girls, I mean *women*, working First Class were astonishingly professional, and I envied their skills. Other than the chain-smoking bovine next to me, all the First Class passengers were males, and the cabin crew called them by name. The F/As smiled a lot and flirted just a little and I sure as hell wasn't going to be able to do this. Perhaps not even in economy. If I survived Training, perhaps I could hide in the galley.

Or an aft lavatory.

There wasn't much of a headwind and we pierced American airspace a half an hour ahead of schedule. We circled for an hour in a holding pattern before we were given our clearance to land at JFK. Once on the ground, we taxied for what seemed halfway to Cleveland and finally pulled up to our gate. As we deplaned, the First Class purser shot me a warm smile and squeezed my arm. Was I really going to get to work for Pan Am? And fly to the four corners of the world? With *women* like this?

Pan Am had no domestic routes (e.g., New York to Miami), so I changed planes at JFK and flew down to San Juan on a 707. Most of the flight attendants were Hispanic, and the plane was packed with large families and screaming children. I had never seen so much carry-on luggage come on an airplane before. One passenger came on with a small television. Someone else brought a cello onboard. Yet someone else had the heaviest hanging bag I had ever seen and he had to drag it down the aisle. A dead relative?

The passengers all looked like the street gang the "Sharks" in *West Side Story*, some without the scars and wounds from sharp instruments. The announcements were made in Spanish and we descended into San Juan's *Aeropuerto Internacional Luis Muñoz Marín* in the middle of a heavy downpour and touched down with a steamy puff of burnt rubber on runway 10/28, complete with zig-zag shards of lightning and full percussion session. Upon deplaning, I was surprised to note that Pan Am could afford to let so many passengers take the blankets and pillows with them. There was no jet-bridge and when the front door was opened a tropical wave of humidity stormed in. I made a mental note to avoid the Caribbean in the summer months—if I lived through Training, that is.

I changed planes again in San Juan, and flew a bucking bronco of a 727 into Miami International Airport through a scrotum-shriveling electrical storm with ear-bleeding thunder.

By the time I arrived, I was tired, sweaty, frightened and really excited.

I took my "transfer voucher" and gave it to a taxicab driver who did not speak English, and he drove me over to the Traveler's Motel on NW 36th Street. I checked in and was relieved when they actually had a reservation for me. I was given a room on the ground floor with two beds. I placed my suitcase on the bed closest to the window, flung back the curtains and looked out. Wow! An Eastern Air Lines L-1011 was taking off right in front of my face, and I could hear the roar of its engines.

There was a window A/C unit, juddering, making almost as much noise as the L-1011. I dropped the A/C down a notch, showered, changed into fresh clothes and headed down to the lobby. I was in Class 4, of 1973. Classes 1, 2, and 3 of 1973 were hunkered down in the moderately more up-market Miami Airways Hotel, farther up NW 36th Street, to the west.

Just off the lobby of our motel was a coffee shop and dining room. I wondered why the dining room had a scale in it. I did a little tour. The motel had a small, moody bar and a swimming pool with what appeared to be no shallow end.

When I returned to the lobby, I noticed two wide-eyed souls like myself sitting there. One was Stanford Oliver, the other Rob Halkides. We introduced ourselves.

"Stan" had been hired out of Dallas, and he often, cheekily, slipped into a posh Scottish lilt. Fluent in Spanish and Portuguese, and annoyingly competent in German, he was also a maven of Scottish Gaelic.

Rob had been hired out of LA, spoke fluent Russian, passable Serbian, was a fountain of knowledge, and laughed a lot.

Stan and Rob were exceedingly affable, switched-on, and I knew right off I was among superior intellect.

We hit the coffee shop, procured a cup of vile coffee and pulled out a list of names we'd been given. It was a list of our soon-to-be classmates. We scoured the list.

We read through the names and tried to envision what our new colleagues would look like. Wendy Shepherd...*fox*. Janie Hulton...*fox*. Carrie Thomas...*fox*. Vilhelmiina Venäläinen... *Finnish*.

It was hot and humid, even for January. Stan and Rob wanted to go for a swim. I repaired to my room to get my cowabunga baggies and opened the door. Unpacking his suitcase onto the other bed was my new roommate, the Inbred Roomie From Hell. I will not give you his Christian or surname, so as not to implicate him for the racist schmuck he was. Inbred Roomie From Hell looked up at me and uttered: "Afraid I was gonna get a black one."

"Excuse me?"

"I'm just joshin' with you," he said.

Inbred Roomie From Hell hailed from the backwater bayous of Louisiana and spoke both German and French, as did I, but I never could understand his voodoo French or his curious southern-Louisiana German patois.

Indeed, I didn't understand anything about IRFH, at all.

****NOTE OF FLEETING IMPORT**: (Residents of German descent comprise Louisiana's largest cultural group. Many came from the historically disputed Alsace-Lorraine region, which helps to explain the easy assimilation of French and German customs. Some historians credit these German farmers with the survival of early New Orleans).

To my horror, I would soon learn that IRFH was the most overt and vocally racist/sexist/misogynist, flaming bigot I had ever encountered in my life. When I confronted him about this, he maintained that he loved all minorities and he was just joking. And then he would make another disparaging remark.

11

Terror in the Classroom

It was muggy and already shirt stick-to-your-back hot when we were loaded into a little white bus with a light-blue "CREW" stenciled on its side at 7.15am the next morning. Despite the heat, I was simply thrilled that the bus said "CREW" and not "DADE COUNTY DEPARTMENT OF CORRECTIONS".

We were transferred to the Pan Am Training School for Flight Attendants. It was located on the north side of Miami International Airport, just off NW 36th Street, in Miami Springs, and it was an architectural marvel. We were told that it was a replica of the American Embassy in New Delhi. I didn't know it at the time, but just over five weeks later I would be standing in New Delhi, gazing upon the very building that inspired it.

**AUTHOR'S MILDLY INTERESTING NOTE: The American Embassy in New Delhi was designed by architect Edward D. Stone. Stone had also been the architect of the Kennedy Center for the Performing Arts in Washington, D.C. At the time, Edward Stone won the commission for the American Embassy with his bold concept of "the best in South Asian architecture, blended with modern Western concepts."

No easy feat.

Frank Lloyd Wright called it "One of the finest buildings in the last hundred years."

Pan Am called our version "The best training facility for flight attendants in the world."

Our first day of Training began promptly at 8am, and we all came dressed in business attire. I took a seat right up front. I didn't want to miss anything. Plus, if I were ever called upon by one of our instructors, I wouldn't have to endure a whole class swiveling around in their seats eyeing me in the back row. The word SMILE was written on the chalkboard, but I didn't need to be reminded, I was beaming from ear to ear.

Our three instructors were introduced. An attractive redhead with short hair (whose name I can't recall), a twenty-something Japanese/American fellow (whose name I can't recall). And Diane Roberts (whose name I will *never* forget. *Ever*).

Diane Roberts was blonde, attractive, intelligent and exceedingly charming. And she scared the living shit out of us. She never showed it, but we all sensed it: "You did not want to fuck up around Diane Roberts."

Diane spoke words of wisdom, words which went something like: "This is the first day of your new life. This is a new career. And it's a new lifestyle. You will never be the same. We are strict. Be punctual. Better too early than too late. If you work for an airline and you're late, your place of employment flies off to another country. Training School will be the best of times; however, for some of you, it will be the worst of times." Not verbatim, mind you, but that was the gist/threat.

And we were warned some of us would not survive Training. We would simply be called out of class, we would have to retreat to the motel, humiliated tail between scrawny, quivering legs, pack up, and disappear.

"Never *assume* anything," Diane Roberts told us, as she scrawled the word on the chalkboard. "Remember, the word 'assume' makes an *ass* out of *u* and *me*."

Yikes, Diane Roberts had a way of being charming *and* intimidating all at the same time.

We were given our manual, which was about as mind-numbing as the Magna Carta and as thick as the original stone-inscribed Ten Commandments (and as heavy), and told in no uncertain terms that we were not to lose it. *Or else*. Visions of being told we "would be swung about by the testicles" if we lost the manual flash into my mind as I write this, but I don't think that was the actual threat (what with there being females in the class), plus, the threat would have been much more intimidating than that.

About now, Training School started to become a surrealistic, roller-coaster blur, a fuzzy blur of terror and fatigue, hope and loads of despair. Somewhere in here, we were given an ID, filled out a bunch of forms, had our passports scrutinized by someone who resembled the Austrian actor Markovics in the movie *The Counterfeiters*, and were told if there was ever a crash we would not be permitted to talk to the media (if we survived). I believe we signed a release regarding that. Not the surviving, the talking.

* * *

We were given a surprisingly thorough physical examination. Had our height measured. And our weight taken. For my height, I could not weigh over 167 pounds. I stepped on the scale and my eyes grew stalks. My weight was 171! How could that be? I worked out. I trained. I watched what I ate, religiously. I didn't smother my French fries with mayo, or go for that extra slice of deep-dish pizza, or eat chocolate chip cookie dough...cold...very often. Nurse Ratched was doing the weigh-in and she was shaking her head at me in a "poor dumb schmuck" sort of way. She had a hammer and chisel in her hands and was just about to etch in stone "171 pounds" and sound the death knell, when I heard laughter. I glanced behind me. Both Stan Oliver and Rob Halkides were shitting themselves. I looked down. Rob had his foot on the back of the scale, pressing it gently and gleefully down. I was re-weighed. My weight: 164 pounds. I let go with a sigh of relief, then muttered "164!"

"That's right, Juanito," Stan Oliver said. "You're only a fat chili-cheese burrito away from being sent home."

We had to have 20-20 vision. Correctable. So we had an eye test. My English classmates called the letter Z, "zed" and received funny looks from the examiner. Vilhelmiina Venäläinen had never done an eye test in English and wondered where the umlauts were. These were minor cultural differences that could be exceedingly amusing or terrifying at the time. One classmate was dyslexic, but eidetic, and passed no problem.

Then we were X-rayed, presumably to see if we were harboring a creature like in the movie *Alien*. And we had our blood pressure checked. Some of my classmates had white-coat phobia, and their blood pressure rocketed frighteningly off the charts. Ruth, who had been a trained nurse back in Switzerland, suggested that instead of taking the blood pressure right at the start of the medical examination, when we were all stressed, take it at the end when we had settled down a bit. This technique was adopted and everyone passed with flying colours.

* * *

When it was time for the Customer Service part of Training, we all looked at it as a welcomed break. Hadn't we been hired on account of being personable and smiley and, well, naturals at what was the foundation of customer service? Were we ever wrong! We were chastised for touching the wine glass with the bottle, for not serving the passenger by the window first, for not offering wine with every meal, for not doing the "CLIPPER DIP." Everyone in class took turns playing passengers or cabin attendants…and we somehow found it all just a bit embarrassing.

About now, we learned that two prospective flight attendants had been sent packing. One in Class 2 and one in Class 3. They were called out of the middle of their classes and just "vanished."

****BIT OF DIRT NOTE**: One candidate was sent home for doing blow just outside the classroom. Yes, you heard right. The other for having sex al fresco. Further details such as location/position were not forthcoming.

With the spectre of dismissal constantly hanging over our heads, and a well-stocked bar just a short hop from our motel room, it was very tempting to spend some quality time in there to relieve the tension. But most of us didn't. Especially the foreign candidates. They were not only struggling with everything we had to learn in "the manual," many were struggling mightily with English. Specifically, a young lady from Germany. It wasn't going well for her, so some of us who spoke German helped. We went to her room and translated the tricky stuff, we coached her and quizzed her, and we soothed her feverish Teutonic brow. She told us that she was desperate to pass and become a flight attendant. She had dreamed about it ever since she was a little girl and flew with her parents from West Berlin to Munich, utilizing Pan Am's Internal German Service, the IGS. She told us there was not great opportunity for women in 1972/73 in Bavaria, and she didn't want to end up working in one of Munich's iconic beer halls such as the Hofbräuhaus (*"In München steht ein Hofbräuhaus, oans, zwoa, g'suffa!"*) or the Mathäser (1450 seats), as many of her buxom schoolmates had done. We were really rooting for her. We were one big family on a fast moving ship that could hit an iceberg at any moment, and we were all doing everything we could to steer clear of danger.

To calm her nerves, our young German colleague ate like there was no tomorrow, which for her was a distinct possibility—and she was putting on weight. As soon as we discovered this, we would roust her from her sleep and run her up and down 36th Street a few times. She hated the jogging so much, she finally gained control of her voracious eating habits and ceased and desisted being a mindless eating machine.

The stress took a toll on our fingernails and they were a mess. Those of us who had never bit our nails in our life, started to neurotically gnaw on them when we got to Training School. So, now, besides watching our weight, we would have to watch our fingernails grow.

The Training School had a full mock-up galley, and it was here we learned how to create exquisite gourmet meals, cook a roast beef the size of a beaver and eggs to order for First Class passengers. About now, while, curiously, I was producing the offending *green* eggs, the door to our classroom sprang open, and a rather severe looking man stuck his head in. We all froze.

This gentleman had a bit of the look of an executioner about him. He studied us all, and to my horror said: "Jon Breakfield?"

I put my tongs down and raised my hand.

"Will you come with me, please. Not questioned—*stated*.

I just about dropped dead. *What had I done wrong?* I was being hauled out of the class and I was going to be dumped from Training. Back to the hotel, pack your bags, "CREW" bus to the airport, handed a ticket.

Never to be a flight attendant.

Never to fly with Pan Am.

Dream shattered.

Waster.

Loser.

All my classmates watched me as I was led from the room, a tableau of shock, stunned silent by impending, life-changing doom. The severe man guided me down the hall to the medical examining rooms. I was ushered in. A doctor and nurse were in there, looking very solemn and just a bit morose, I thought.

"Have a seat," the doctor said.

No problem, I thought, *I'm shitting a brick and you want me to have a seat*.

"We've just been studying your X-rays..." he began. "You have a slightly enlarged heart and your pulse is uncharacteristically low. Afraid we're going to have to send you home."

I looked at the doctor, then the nurse, then the severe man, who didn't seem quite so severe now, rather more compassionate and avuncular.

"Excuse me?"

"We're sending you home..."

"I was a runner," I muttered.

"Pardon?"

"I was a long distance runner in high school and on the track team in college. I'm not in poor health," I said in my defense, "I have an athlete's heart. If anything, I'm really fit."

The doctor took the stethoscope off from around his neck, blew on it to warm it and stuck it on my quivering chest. He asked me to do a series of vigorous jumping jacks. Quickly, he took my pulse.

"Your pulse is returning to normal as I'm checking it! Never seen anything like it. There's nothing wrong with you. Now get back to class before you miss anything important."

Oh my God. I was so relieved. That had scared the bleeping hell out of me.

* * *

Everyone in our class got along famously—except four individuals. These four were technicolor nightmares, and we all wondered how they had been hired in the first place. They had taken the jobs out of the desperate mitts of four others who would have gladly donated an organ to be part of Pan Am. My Roomie From Hell was one of the four. A radiant racist who had no right being anywhere else other than in solitary confinement, with the key thrown away or melted down. Then there were two slinky model types from Sydney, and a lone male deviate from the Netherlands. The two model types were in love with themselves. Not each other, mind you, just themselves. They ended up hating the airline business so much that shortly after Training School (now that they had visas and were based in New York), they quit and went to work at Macy's selling make-up. Then there was the pervert from the Netherlands, he completely unnerved his roommate, Simon, from England. Apparently, Mr. Dutch Deviate would just sit on his bed, in the Lotus position, chain smoking, watching Simon sleep. Of course, Simon was afraid what would happen to him if he actually ever drifted off and was becoming a zombie, and one of the few Pan Am candidates who hoped he would survive Training and get out on the line where he could finally garner some quality sleep, which of course didn't exist.

When the grooming part of Training began, we initially treated it as a PHEWWW relief. Hadn't we been hired at least partly on account of our appearance? Grooming was when we realized that everything about our appearance was wrong. Presumably correctable, but worryingly wrong. Everyone's hair was too long, or too curly or too flat, or too stylish or not stylish enough. And I'm not talking about the women yet.

One of Vidal Sassoon's male scissor-sisters galumphed up one day and had a go at Janie Hulton's long brunette locks. Janie was absolutely game, and patently mortified, and when it was all over, decidedly chuffed. And we all had to say, she looked quite the flight attendant. Vidal Sassoon offered Pan Am discounts at the time, and from then on, I had my hair clipped at one of their salons near Slone Square, on the boundaries of central London's Knightsbridge, Belgravia and Chelsea districts. When I entered Sassoon's, I was always afforded a friendly greeting when I showed my Pan Am I.D., and all the staff were curious about what exotic locations I had been flying to. (I would always be amazed at how much respect we were afforded all over the world by *being* Pan Am.) It didn't hurt that it was the dead of winter in London, it was starting to get dark at 3.15 in the afternoon, and I always came in deeply tanned from my trips to Africa, Beirut, India and Bangkok. It was just one of the many perks of working for Pan Am—Vidal Sassoon *and* the tan.

* * *

During Training, we learned the crucial fact that one of the first individuals to arrive at a crash scene was—a painter. Yes, a painter, and he arrived there fast (obviously non-union). Many image-conscious airlines immediately dispatched a painter to the smoldering wreckage so he could paint over what was left of the company's logo. This way, when the predacious journalists arrived moments later, and started snapping and rolling, the airline's name and logo would not be splashed across the front pages and T.V. screens of the world.

And it was during our Training School days that we heard our first airline joke: We heard that our worldly international carrier was going to merge with a little unsophisticated puddle-jumper of a feeder airline. It was well known within the industry at the time that the little feeder airline hired stewardesses according to the size of their breasts rather than the size of their brains. The going joke was that after the merger we would teach them how to pour wine and they would teach us how to chew gum.

12

The Best Airline in the World

As the runaway locomotive that was Training School sped on at a break-neck pace, we learned Pan Am flight routes, world geography, and airport 3-letter call signs. We learned about what kept an airplane up in the air. What to do if it fell out of the sky. We committed to memory the range of each aircraft. Its fuel capacity. Its wingspan. Its seating configuration. Where all the life rafts, oxygen, First Aid kits and fire extinguishers were stowed and, just to keep us on our toes, how it was completely different between 727s, 707s and 747s.

We committed to memory everything we could about Boeing 727s: mid-size narrow-body tri-engine (3 Pratt & Whitney JT8D turbofans), had a cockpit crew of 3, and could carry 149 to 189 passengers. They could take off on shorter runways at smaller airports, climb quicker and were noisy as hell. They were intended for short- to medium-range flights, and depending on take-off weight had a range of roughly 2,500 miles. They could, in a perfect world, zoom along at 600 miles per hour and had a ceiling of 40,000 feet, give or take.

I found it interesting that the 727 was actually in operation at this time for the "IGS," the Internal German Service, the routes our German classmate first flew on as a young girl. Pan Am operated short-haul scheduled service between West Germany and West Berlin. The IGS was formed at the end of World War II upon agreement between the United States, the United Kingdom, the Soviet Union and France. Since Germany, for obvious reasons, was prohibited from having its own airline, someone needed to get folk in and out of West Berlin.

And that was Pan Am.

In the days of the Iron Curtain, there were only three air

corridors into the "island" that West Berlin had become, and the three corridors extended over communist East Germany. Since the Allies controlled three occupation zones: American, British and French, there was one airline for each zone: BEA (later merged with BOAC to become British Airways), Air France, and Pan Am. To ensure that the lives of the pilots and passengers would be miserable and in constant jeopardy, the communist powers-that-be had imposed an altitude restriction through these meteorologically mercurial corridors of just 10,000 feet. This translated to shitty weather in winter, zero visibility, and bowel-evacuating turbulence. In spring, summer and autumn, it oft translated to shitty weather, zero visibility, and bowel-evacuating turbulence, as well.

**AUTHOR'S SOMEWHAT INTERESTING TIDBIT: (Years later, I would return to Kitzbühel, Austria, where I had first learned the German language, and I would meet a group of Pan Am pilots who lived in Kitzbühel and flew in the IGS or were New York-based: John Hinkle, Jim McFarlane, Mayhugh Horne, Patrick Dwyer, and Charlie Matthews. A great group of pilots, and all damn good skiers.)

And then there was the 707. The 707s were mid-size, long-range, narrow-bodies. The 707 could seat 140 to 219 passengers, *más o menos*, and had a range from 2,500 miles to 5,750.

The "Seven-Oh-Seven" was Boeing's first jetliner, and was the first to usher in the true Jet Age—and the Jet Set. Before they were able to employ private jets, the rich-and-famous Jet Set flew almost exclusively Pan Am First Class.

In October of 1958, Pan Am and the 707 made history by inaugurating the first 707 service and the first daily transatlantic jet service from New York to Paris. Once in Paris, it was just a short hop down to the topless and nude-beach playgrounds of the French Rivera: St. Tropez, Cannes, Juan-les-Pins, Cap d'Antibes, Antibes, Nice, Villefranche, Saint-Jean-Cap Ferrat and Menton. And let's not forget the baccarat (*punto banco*) and black jack tables and roulette wheels of Monte Carlo.

Then there was the 747. The "Seven-Four." When we saw our first 747 while we were standing on the tarmac, mouths open, gazing up at it with reverence and possibly just a bit of childlike wonder, we were stunned to learn it was over a three-story drop from the emergency door of the upper deck, or from the cockpit. If an emergency occurred while on the ground, and the cockpit crew had to evacuate through the escape hatch, they grabbed one of the five inertia reels and abseiled down, all very Spiderman like.

In April 1966, Pan Am placed an order with Boeing for twenty-five 747s at a cool price of $21 million each (today, one will set you back over $200 million, if you want all the bells and whistles). The 747 is so reliable, it can safely fly for 16 or more hours per day. "Keep the planes in the air," was the game plan for success.

To put the glorious jumbo in perspective, the wingspan of a 747 varies from 195 feet 8 inches to 224 feet 7 inches. If that doesn't mean anything to you, chomp on this: The Wright Brothers first flight at Kill Devil Hills, near Kitty Hawk, NC, lasted 12 seconds and could have been completed on the wing of a 747.

With room to spare.

The 747 would not have come about if Juan Trippe hadn't had his vision of mass air travel over international routes. Trippe convinced his old industry colleague and friend Bill Allen (who was head of Boeing) to construct a much larger aircraft, an aircraft that could seat 2.5 times the number of passengers as a 707.

Trippe said these words to Bill Allen: "If you build it, I'll buy it." Bill Allen rightly responded with: "I'll build it, if you buy it."

For those of you taking notes, it was Juan Terry Trippe who gave the 747 its signature hump. Trippe suggested that the cockpit should be located in an "upper deck" area, so the nose, below, could be opened to accommodate those jumbos that were to be used for cargo.

In order to place the 747 into production, Boeing had to

build the world's largest hangar, and it became the world's largest enclosed space. New engines had to be designed to accommodate the 747, and airport runways and taxiways around the world had to be lengthened, strengthened and widened. Even terminals and jet-bridges had to be redesigned and enlarged.

* * *

Besides the different aircraft we would be flying on, we learned that passenger oxygen masks were useless in combating smoke in the cabin, as they also drew in the toxic air. A damp handkerchief was much better protection. Had you known that? I hadn't known that. We learned that there were CO_2 extinguishers and foam extinguishers and dry chemical extinguishers and water extinguishers. The dry chemical was to be used in the cockpit if there was an electrical fire. Only the year before an ill-advised effort had been exacted by a flight attendant who used a water extinguisher…on an *electrical* fire…in the cockpit. While the cockpit crew donned smoke hoods, the eager F/A burst in and gave the flight deck and all its electrical components a jolly good dousing.

And, no, it wasn't Pan Am.

We knew better.

I won't mention the offending airline on these pages so as not to disparage the gum-chewing cabin attendants.

* * *

In Training School, during Emergency (hell) Week, we were shown "THE FILM." The scare-the-bejesus-out-of-you film about an incident which occurred in October of 1956. A Pan Am Boeing Stratocruiser, Clipper *Sovereign of the Skies*, was enroute from Honolulu to San Francisco, on the final leg of its scheduled around-the-world flight. Flight 6 had just passed "The Point of No Return," (in actuality, this is known as PET "the Point of Equal Time" as it factors in winds aloft, the time to limp back to the departure airport and/or the time to carry on bravely toward the destination airport). About now, the first officer was less than thrilled to notice that the number one engine was over-revving. When the propeller wouldn't feather, Captain "Dick" Ogg forced the engine to stop by cutting off its oil supply. This killed the RPMs, the engine seized, but the propeller continued to windmill. This placed significant drag on the aircraft, and immense problems for Captain Ogg.

And then things got worse.

The Stratocruiser began to lose altitude. At a rate of 1,000 feet per minute, not so good as it was only cruising at 21,000 feet at the time. To maintain altitude, Captain Ogg added power to the remaining three engines.

Then the number four engine began to act up, it backfired, backfired again, kept on backfiring, and the propeller on the engine had to be feathered.

The flight from Honolulu to San Francisco was estimated to take 8 hours, 54 minutes. Captain Ogg had the airplane fueled for a flight time of 12 hours 18 minutes, but now on the two remaining engines they were only doing 140 knots, and there was no way they would make San Francisco, and they couldn't return to Honolulu without running out of fuel.

Down on the surface of the ocean, halfway between the Hawaiian Islands and the coast of California, at a designated point known as "Ocean Station November," a Coast Guard cutter gunboat cleaved the shimmering Pacific, making lazy circles and figure eights, holding its position. This was the 255-foot USCGC *Pontchartrain*, used as a weather ship and, in case of emergency, there to assist those in distress.

Captain Ogg made contact with the *Pontchartrain*, explained his dilemma and asked about current weather conditions. The *Pontchartrain* came back with these words: "The seas are running swells at five feet, wind out of the northwest at eight knots."

Captain Ogg had to make an immediate executive decision: he decided to set the *Sovereign of the Skies* down on the ocean, but was concerned about loss of life with still so much fuel onboard. There could be an explosion and subsequent fire. That, plus half-full tanks of fuel would weigh the aircraft down and it would sink more rapidly.

Captain Ogg was able to level off and maintain altitude at just 2,000 feet, so he decided to fly through the night, circling near the *Pontchartrain*, endeavouring to burn fuel, and hoping like hell there would be no further problems with the two remaining engines. It wasn't in the film, but I bet he was also hoping for those seas running at five feet to flatten down a bit. I can't even imagine the stress and terror for those onboard that night.

By now, Juan Trippe, back in New York, was following the events as they unfolded. Trippe had Pan Am's Chief Engineer John Borger contact Boeing in Seattle, and Boeing suggested positioning all the passengers over the wings for the ditching. Boeing knew from a previous ditching that the tail section of the Stratocruiser would split and break apart on impact.

Until first light, the *Sovereign of the Skies* circled the weather ship, making eight-mile patterns. The crew of the *Pontchartrain* laid down a "runway of foam," to mark the course, and as dawn broke bright and clear, Captain Ogg positioned his aircraft for the "water landing." The crippled Stratocruiser made one practice pass, did a 360, came in low and slow (just 104 miles per hour) and parallel to the weather ship. As she touched the surface of the ocean, bits and pieces of the 17-feet-in-diameter props flew in the air, she hit a large swell with the left wing, lurched violently and broke apart. Immediately the tail section sank, yet within two minutes, the stewardess, purser and cockpit crew had all the passengers in life rafts and arriving lifeboats, some having simply walked across the wing, never even getting wet.

Captain Ogg and the purser were the last to leave Clipper *Sovereign of the Skies*.

Twenty minutes later, Clipper *Sovereign of the Skies*, sank into her watery grave.

A few crew members of the *Pontchartrain* had filmed the entire event, and we sat there in Training School, stunned, yet impressed, with the textbook ditching emblazoned on our brains.

And may I take pause to honour and remember our Pan Am confrères on duty that autumn day back in 1956:

Captain Richard "Dick" Ogg, age 43.
First Officer George Haaker, age 40.
Navigator Richard Brown, age 31.
Flight Engineer Frank Garcia, Jr., age 30.
Purser Patricia Reynolds, age 30.
Stewardess Mary Ellen Daniel, age 24.
Stewardess Katherine Araki, age 23.

The Stratocruiser 377 was a double-deck aircraft. Located on the upper deck were the flight deck, passenger cabin and galley. Down below, there was a lounge and cargo area. The Stratocruiser was pressurized, had a cruising speed of 301 miles per hour and a maximum speed of 375 miles per hour. Its service ceiling was 32,000 feet, its range 4,200 miles. The 377 could be configured to carry up to 100 passengers, or 28 in sleeping births.

****AUTHOR'S NOTE**: Here's the link of the film footage of that harrowing day dutifully compiled by the crack USCG: https://www.youtube.com/watch?v=XvagZxur7sU

* * *

Pan Am became the first airline to have cabin attendants, first to serve meals in the air, first to build airfields hacked out of jungle and volcanic rock, first to navigate by instruments, first to be able to inform their pilots exactly where they were at all times, first to develop a complete aviation weather service and long-range weather forecasting, first to fly across the Pacific, first to fly across the Atlantic, and the first to fly around the world.

Pan Am even knew how to ditch an aircraft and get it right.

All under the incomparable guidance, genius and vision of Juan Terry Trippe.

PART II

13

A Young Boy

Let me temporarily interrupt my harrowing, yet gloriously memorable time at Training School for a moment and give you a peek at some back story. This eye-watering, eye-opening information has never been documented in its entirety.

In September of 1909, a group called the Hudson-Fulton Celebration Commission had planned on the Wright Brothers being in attendance to fly exhibition flights to help mark 300 years of New York and New Jersey history. This included the 300th anniversary of Henry Hudson's discovery of the "Hudson River," and the 100th anniversary of Robert Fulton's paddle steamer. The commission was made up of an impressive rich man's gallery of influential New Yorkers, the likes of J.P. Morgan and Andrew Carnegie. As an aircraft in flight was novel and thrilling to observe, the commission wanted Orville and Wilbur to "perform flight demonstrations," and they wanted them to do something risky that hadn't been attempted on this side of the Atlantic: *fly over water*. At the last moment, it was learned that Orville was delayed in Germany and unable to attend. The Celebration Commission was keen to generate great publicity for the occasion, so if they couldn't get Orville, they would go after someone who—when matched up against Wilbur Wright—would garner even more publicity: Glenn Curtiss, the Wright Brothers' dastardly arch rival.

The "runway"—for what was scheduled to be a feisty barnstorming competition—was the soft, sand-covered parade ground on Governors Island in Upper New York Bay. Glenn Curtiss had just arrived from an air demonstration in Rheims,

France, the day before, and was dismayed to learn that his business partner, without getting the okay from him, had signed a contract for the princely sum of $9,000 to display his faithful "Rheims airplane" in the Wanamaker and Filene's department stores in Manhattan for the next two months! (Curtiss' business partner was inspired when he had seen a flying machine on display at Selfridges in London, *indoors*.)

Suddenly, Curtiss had to scramble for a substitute aircraft (not so easy in those days, aeroplanes were few and far between) and could only come up with an inferior piece of machinery with little in the way of engine power, flight stability, or demonstration capability.

For the first few days of the exhibition, the weather did not behave, and when the pilots were finally able to take to the skies, Curtiss' flimsy substitute airplane's thin wheels bogged down in the soft sand of Governors Island as he endeavored to take off. After much effort, and just a bit of luck, he was able to get his craft in the air, but almost immediately he fought fierce crosswinds and had to set back down after travelling no more than 300 meters.

This is not what the large crowd had come for.

Wright seized the chance to stick it to his nemesis by cleverly forgoing wheels and affixing a canoe beneath the fuselage to act as a pontoon in case he needed to ditch. To deal with the heavy sand, he eschewed wheels and cleverly took off on thin skids into a headwind. He made a short test flight, circling the island to ensure the canoe would not adversely affect the airplane's performance. Pleased with the plane's stability, he took off again and flew—*over water*—past the four funnels of the departing Cunard liner R.M.S. *Lusitania* (which would be sunk by a German U-boat six years later) and a flotilla of other watercraft, one mile to the Statue of Liberty. Many onlookers feared he would crash into Lady Liberty as he approach her at only "knee height" (the top of the torch is 305 feet), but he indeed carved a neat turn around her once shackled feet, then flew back completing a figure eight and landed into the wind on the sandy parade ground of

Governors Island on those trusty skids.

The flight itself and the ensuing bickering with Glenn Curtiss caused quite a sensation in the press the next day and much-needed publicity was indeed generated, that *plus* the "lighting of New York City" was taking place. Town halls and museums were dressed with lights and illuminated, as was the Statue of Liberty, Grant's Tomb, the Washington Arch, and the Brooklyn Bridge. The city was literally electrified with the addition of 500,000 incandescent light bulbs.

This celebration was a big, big deal.

A few days later, Wright again piloted his plane, the "Flyer," with two American flags fluttering proudly from the front canard and another from the canoe, past the Statue of Liberty. He was going to stick it to Glenn Curtiss all over again by fulfilling the promise that Curtiss had made but couldn't keep: a flight right on up the Hudson River—all over water—to Grant's Tomb and back, flying over a prodigious fleet of ships from all over the world.

And this is what Wilbur Wright did.

For 33 minutes, he soared at 200 feet over the Hudson as ships sounded their horns, trolleys clanged their bells, cars honked, and folk wildly cheered him on his record-setting way. He fought vicious thermal currents yet still managed to fly a thousand feet past Grant's Tomb. All this in front of more than a million cheering spectators, who had lined both sides of the Hudson.

Standing among those cheering spectators with his father was a ten-year-old star-struck boy—Juan Terry Trippe.

And he was immediately and forever smitten with the art of flying.

* * *

I was fascinated with Juan Trippe and I wanted to know more about what made the man, motivated him, and drove him to become the most visionary leader in aviation the world had ever known. I did some digging around to augment what we had learned in Training School:

Juan Terry Trippe was born in 1899 in the quaint beach town of Sea Bright, New Jersey, into what was believed to be a family of considerable wealth. Despite the Hispanic Christian name, he was actually of English roots, his seafaring ancestors stemming from Canterbury in Kent, England.

But that was just the father's side of the family.

Stay with me now as I introduce you to a certain Irish "colleen" with strawberry blonde ringlets and deep dimples by the name of Katherine Louise Flynn, or Kitty Flynn, as she was known to all involved. Kitty was from the slums of Dublin, Ireland, born into a life of dire deprivation, and she wanted out. She desired life's finer things…she wanted to be a "society lady."

By the age of 17, Kitty was stunningly attractive, keen of wit, had a body to die for, and was working as a barmaid in the decidedly down-market taproom of the Washington Hotel in Liverpool. A year later, she made the acquaintance of a pair of rich Americans who claimed to be businessmen, Adam Worth and Charles Bullard (aka "Piano Charley"). But things weren't as they seemed. Adam Worth was the most ingenious, cerebral and remarkable super-criminal known in modern times. He had cheekily assumed the name of a dead man, Henry Jarvis Raymond, who just happened to have been the editor and co-founder of the *New York Times*, then Worth changed the middle name so he became Henry "Judson" Raymond.

His sidekick Piano Charley was a career criminal and at the top of his game, but nowhere near the ilk of Adam Worth. Worth was the ultimate master at pickpocketing, art theft, safe cracking, international check forgery, swindling, larceny, bank robbery, jewelry store robbery, diamond theft, mail robbery, burglary, even roadway hold ups. All this, and yet he was not a violent man. Indeed, he abhorred violence. His weapon of choice was his intellect. He would remind his gang of thieving associates time and time again of what had become his code of ethics by which to live: "A man with brains has no right to carry firearms. Exercise your brain!" Adam Worth never threatened anyone. Never bullied anyone. He even gave food and rent money to criminals at the bottom of the thieving totem pole who were on the down and out. He didn't want the dosh returned, just loyalty. And loyalty he received.

Adam Worth preferred to steal from the rich, those "who could afford to lose a small piece of the pie."

And in doing so he became one of the most *respected* men in all of Europe.

In many ways he was a modern-day Robin Hood.

Both Adam Worth and Piano Charley Bullard courted Kitty and she slept with them both, repeatedly, and she continued to do so even after she married Bullard. When things started to go pear-shaped for the trio in Liverpool, they picked up sticks and scarpered 500 miles south to Paris where they bought an abandoned three-story building with some of the $200,000 Worth and Bullard had left over from when they'd robbed the vault of the Boylston National Bank in Boston by digging a tunnel from a neighbouring shop, all too aware that the Pinkerton Detective Agency already had them in its crosshairs.

Out of the vast structure of the abandoned building, they built a palatial nightclub called the American Bar, at 2, Rue Scribe (and not far from the Paris Opera House), in the 9th arrondissement, complete with American newspapers and magazines, and American barmen, and a second-floor "clubhouse" where American ex-pats could hangout and even receive mail from back home. The floors above the clubhouse contained a casino which catered to well-heeled socialites, wealthy bankers, royalty—and all the scum in between: forgers, art thieves, cat burglars, convicts, counterfeiters, con men...and many an *entitled* wayward royal.

Since gambling was illegal in Paris, the gambling tables and roulette wheels were designed so that they could be quickly folded away and secreted inside the walls and floors at the press of a warning buzzer. The American Bar carried such a lofty reputation, it even caught the attention of the officers of the Boylston National Bank in Boston on the other side of the pond and they made a surprise "jolly" to the chic venue to party and recharge the batteries, unaware that the club had been financed by the loot stolen from their very own institution.

Kitty had a way with people, and she played hostess at the casino, openly flirted, and charmed the American Bar's affluent clientele. Everyone sought her company. Piano Charley entertained the guests by, you guessed it, tickling the ivories.

The reputation of the American Bar continued to spread, and it became the "in" place to go in Paris. In fact, the reputation spread all the way to the Pinkerton Detective Agency back in Chicago.

One evening William Pinkerton himself turned up at the American Bar. And Adam Worth recognized him.

But nothing was said. No action taken.

Shortly thereafter, the bar was summarily raided.

The trio fled back to England, where Adam Worth purchased a stately manor house for himself, Piano Charley and Kitty. The prodigious red-brick, two-story dwelling was called West Lodge, and it sported a private tennis court, bowling green and shooting gallery. Nice digs. It was set on vast grounds and well back from the street and located on London's south side, not far from Wimbledon. Adam Worth had evolved into a cultured gentleman with fine taste, and he had West Lodge furnished with antiques, rare books and fond memorabilia, much of it lifted from the now defunct and shuttered American Bar.

Since he needed time to chill, and spend some quality time alone with Kitty, Adam Worth also set himself up with a bolt hole at 198 Piccadilly, in London's fashionable Mayfair district.

Sometime about now, Piano Charley slipped into the abyss that is alcoholism and Kitty discovered that he was a bigamist. Never content to be number two in any aspect of her life, Kitty took her two daughters and fled back to America and set themselves up in Brooklyn.

Adam Worth was desperate for his paramour Kitty to return to England, and he begged her to come back. He truly loved her—plus, everyone knew that he was the biological father of her two girls, not that old drunk Piano Charley. But Kitty declined, for as quirky fate and the zest for the good life would have it, she had met and fallen for a powerful and prosperous Wall Street banker.

The banker was born in Cuba of Irish-Spanish-Venezuelan descent.

And his name was Juan Pedro Terry y Dorticos.

"Juan Terry," as he was known, was a millionaire, having inherited a fortune from his father, Tomás Terry, who had made his millions in Cuba in banking, imports, the sugar trade, and the slave trade where he bought sick and injured slaves. He then nursed the slaves back to health and sold them on for a substantial profit.

So here's Juan Terry, a highly respectable businessman, marrying Kitty Flynn of dubious repute. Kitty was now able to finally make the move into respectability and she travelled comfortably in the circles of New York's high society. She had learned well in England and Paris.

Juan Terry raised Kitty and Adam Worth's two girls as if they were his own. And then Kitty and Juan had a child between them—"Juanita Teresita." The two girls from Kitty and Adam Worth's union were called Lucy Adeline and Katherine Louise. Lucy Adeline would grow into a cultured and handsome woman and would eventually marry a New York investment banker by the name of Charles White Trippe. They would go on to have three children: Charles White Trippe, Jr., Katherine Louise Trippe, and none other than Juan Terry Trippe.

One summer's day in 1899, the family was travelling by carriage in Sea Bright and were struck by a train at a level crossing. Juan Trippe, who was only one-year-old at the time survived, as did his mother. Two-year-old Charles, Jr., Katherine Louise Terry, and 13-year-old Juanita Teresita were killed instantly.

A few feet difference, or a speedier train, and there would have been no Pan American World Airways.

14

Lineage

Juan Terry Trippe may have been named after his stepgrandfather, but perhaps Juan's business ethics were not so unlike that of his biological grandfather, Adam Worth? It was President Roosevelt, indeed, who, taken with Juan Trippe's charm and bearing, yet intrigued at the same time by his dogged, inexhaustible, sometimes dark business style using his influence within the government, called him "a Yale educated gangster."

**AUTHOR'S CULTURAL NOTE: Adam Worth's notoriety was such, that Arthur Conan Doyle even used him as the inspiration for Sherlock Holmes' archenemy, criminal mastermind Professor Moriarty.

Adam Worth biographer Ben Macintyre also traces the inspiration for Macavity, the Mystery Cat in T. S. Eliot's *Old Possum's Book of Practical Cats* to Doyle's character Moriarty.

Interestingly enough, Andrew Lloyd Webber based his long-running hit musical *Cats* on T.S. Eliot's work, including the character Macavity.

* * *

For those of you desiring more *pure* ancestral lineage (although it is often in the eye of the beholder): Juan Trippe's great, great grandfather (on his father's side) was a naval war hero of unparalled bravery.

Just off Tripoli, in the Mediterranean, and in full command of Gunboat Number 6, *19-year-old* Lieutenant John Trippe aggressively boarded a towering Barbary pirate corsair with ten of his best mates. Outnumbered by the pirates 36 to 11, young John Trippe fought ferociously to the death. Despite being slashed eleven times by pirate sabres, he would not go down, and he dispatched the Turkish pirate captain, and so scared the living you-know-what out of the remaining enemy sailors, they dropped their sabres, threw their bloodied hands in the air, and surrendered.

All of Trippe's men survived to fight another day.

Lieutenant John Trippe's heroism became legendary, and this battle is still talked about as one of the most heroic deeds by a member of the U.S. Navy, *to date*.

Give that some thought.

Then, in the icy winter of 1809, young Trippe took command of the USS *Enterprise* and sailed for the Netherlands. Once in Amsterdam, he conducted lengthy and official negotiations (ran in the family?) and signed trading rights between the United States and the Netherlands, which opened Dutch ports to American shipping.

Sadly, Lieutenant John Trippe died of yellow fever on 9 July, 1810, at sea, en-route from Havana to New Orleans, at the young age of 25. Lieutenant Trippe attained such stature in his short life, the U.S. Navy awarded him the Congressional Medal of Honor and named four ships in his honour.

15

But First, *Radio*

The *Titanic* sank in April of 1912.

Wireless communication had been poor and ships in the vicinity had been slow to respond.

A few months after the sinking of the *Titanic,* the "Radio Act of 1912" was established. It mandated, among other things, that seagoing vessels continuously monitor distress frequencies.

In 1914, WWI broke out.

And Morse code radio operators were suddenly in demand.

Two large schools were opened to teach Morse code. One was at Mare Island, California, north of San Francisco, the other at Harvard University in Cambridge, Massachusetts.

With the fighting raging across Europe, America entered the war in the spring of 1917. Seventeen-year-old Juan Trippe knew that hundreds upon hundreds of pilots would be needed, and he wanted to be ready. He pestered his father about learning to fly.

But his father had vision, as well, and he wanted young Juan to learn everything he could about Morse code and using a radio, *before* he learned to fly.

By the start of the summer, 1917, Juan's father would have seen this very ad for a school, which taught Morse code, and it was close to home: **MARCONI SCHOOL OF INSTRUCTION Classes in Radio Now Open to Gentlemen Desiring to Qualify for Government or Commercial Marine Service. Graduates under no obligation to the Marconi Company. Write "INSTRUCTING ENGINEER NEW YORK CITY EDISON BUILDING. GIVE YOUR AGE. Thorough inspection invited. Write for 96-page manual. Prospective applicants may have personal interviews from 10 A.M. to 10 P.M. Mondays to Fridays."

Juan was sent to the Marconi Institute in the old Edison Building located at 25 Elm Street at the corner of Duane Street in Lower Manhattan.

(**HEAD-SPINNING NOTE**: I tried to find this address on the map, and struggled for a week until I discovered that "Elm Street" no longer exists. It was renamed *Elk* Street in 1939 in honor of the Benevolent and Protective Order of the Elks, New York Lodge #1. Who knew?)

"The Institute"—or the Marconi School of Instruction as some called it—offered day and evening classes in "radio communication and allied vocations" and boasted facilities for nearly 600 students.

It was here that Juan Trippe learned Morse code and then, later that summer, Juan's father shipped young Juan down to Miami to, of all places, the *Curtiss* Flying School (as in Glenn Curtiss, the Wright Brothers' dastardly arch rival) to learn to fly.

That autumn, Juan enrolled at Yale, where he played starting right guard on the freshmen football team. As WWI accelerated, he left Yale in December and enlisted in the Marines with many of his football teammates. Trippe had designs on becoming a combat pilot, but was mildly flummoxed to learn that the Marine Corps did not train pilots. Juan's father used his considerable influence and succeeded in getting Juan transferred out of the Marines and into the Navy so he could attend flight school. But Juan flunked the eye exam and his father had to pull strings to get another eye test by having a word with the Assistant Secretary of the Navy, a certain fellow by the name of Franklin Roosevelt. Fortunately for all of us, Juan Trippe passed his eye exam by memorizing the bottom line, A-E-P-H-T-I-Y, and became a Navy pilot. He soloed in a "Jenny" biplane trainer, flying for 20 minutes around Long Island. He piloted his first flying boat down in Virginia at "Hampton Roads," that body of water north of

Norfolk and south of Newport News. He increased his knowledge of radio, and flew bombers in Pensacola, Florida. Even qualified to fly the bombers at night.

Do you see where this is going?

On 17 June, 1918, Juan graduated from Naval Flight School, Naval Aviator #1806.

Keen to see action, Juan headed back to New York to prepare to embark for Europe, but the war ended.

Juan re-enrolled at Yale and played Ivy League football, but was kicked in the spine and had to have three vertebrae in his back fused together. It was one of the first attempts to perform this delicate surgery. He was in the hospital for three long months, unable to attend classes.

And he spent most of the time thinking about floatplanes, radio, and night flying.

Thinking of what could be.

Juan's father died unexpectedly and Juan, finally recovered from his surgery, returned to Yale and joined the Yale Aero Club. During the summers he came home to New York City and lived with his mother on East 76th Street and worked on Wall Street as a runner and in the cages for Lee, Higginson & Co. The work bored him to tears, for his love was in the sky.

Trippe graduated from Yale at the age of 23, and he felt aviation was the future, and the future was right then and there. In 1922, he heard of an auction taking place down in Philadelphia. He had his eye set on nine single-engine, twin-seat Aeromarine 39B floatplanes. Young Trippe entered a frightfully low bid, but his bid was laughed at, and he went home without the fleet he had hoped for. But Juan Terry Trippe was never a quitter. And he was innately shrewd. And patient. He simply waited a month for the next auction, entered the exact same bid of $500 each—and won. He ended up purchasing seven of the nine available Aeromarines by using a portion of the modest inheritance his father had left him, and he sold stock to the wealthy, former members of the Yale Aero Club. As the principal stock holder, he installed himself as president, general manager and chief pilot.

And he had his first airline: "Long Island Airways."

The seven aircraft were disassembled, loaded into seven railroad cars and shipped up to the old Naval Air Station on Rockaway Beach in Queens. Trippe had rented an abandoned building within reach of the glassy waters of Jamaica Bay, and he and his friends had to reassemble and test-fly the two-seater floatplanes themselves.

What Juan Trippe couldn't have known at the time was just over there across Jamaica Bay was a vast expanse that twenty-plus years down the road would become Idlewild Airport and eventually John F. Kennedy International Airport.

Trippe did the scheduling for his fledgling airline, the marketing, and the bookkeeping. He even cleaned the toilet, schlepped bags and, when pressed, climbed in the cockpit and flew the planes himself. He and his small stable of ex-military pilots offered rides at Coney Island and Fire Island. They would buzz the beach to draw the attention of the sun worshipers, set down on the calm waters behind the sand dunes, and fried New Yorkers would flock to them and queue up just to get the chance to fly in an *aeroplane*.

Imagine.

At the start, Trippe's fledgling airline only availed itself of "beach business," flourishing during the hot summer months. As one of his pilots mused back then: "the most dangerous part of flying was the risk of starving to death."

Pilots started to find alternative work crop dusting, skywriting, aerial mapping, barnstorming and, during Prohibition, bootlegging.

These extra means of income helped the pilots, but it did little for a man trying to run an airline. *Build an airline,* with published routes and, even *schedules.*

America had the world's best railroads—a quarter-million miles—and the railroads served the major cities. Trains were luxurious, fast, reliable, and they conveyed you directly into the city centers. Aeroplanes were cold, noisy bucking broncos, and they conveyed you to farmers' fields way out in the boonies with no way to get downtown.

Flying was not a way to get somewhere when you needed to get somewhere in a hurry. Flying was barnstorming, flying from town to town, landing in cow pastures, taking a passenger up for a ride at the State Fair and far more thrilling than the rollercoaster or the loopty-loop.

In order to increase revenue for his Long Island Airways, Trippe's planes needed to carry more weight, so he rebuilt his fleet so they might accommodate *three* seats, one pilot, two passengers (which meant "couples could fly"). To do this he had to upgrade his Aeromarine's 90-hp Curtiss OX-5 engines to the much more powerful 220-hp French Hispano-Suiza engines. Then he had to remove something called the "reduction drive" so he could down-size the propellers to, are you ready, prevent them from lopping off the floatplane's pontoons. By the way, when you remove the seemingly important reduction drive, you have to run the engines at a higher rev to generate lift. After all this, Trippe had to remove the fuel tanks from inside the fuselage to make more room for the passengers and re-install them on the outside (the fuel tanks, not the passengers). Somehow, Trippe made it all work, the planes didn't blow mid-flight, and he was able to sell excursions to wealthy couples down to Atlantic City, and up to Newport, R.I. He catered to the rich and taxied them from Manhattan out to the Hamptons. He even disassembled one of his planes himself and shipped it down to Honduras, along with a pilot. He had negotiated a contract with the mighty United Fruit Company to deliver—in an hour and a half—important documents from the port in Tela, Honduras, to the capital of Tegucigalpa that were presently taking three days by treacherous road over mountains that rose to beyond 9,000 feet.

And Long Island Airways now had tentacles stretching deep into Central America.

****AUTHOR'S GEOGRAPHIC NOTE**: The United Fruit Company had banana plantations across Central and South America, and maintained such a formidable monopoly in countries like Costa Rica, Honduras and Guatemala, they came to be known as "Banana Republics." Well, I'll be.

Che Guevara was understandably unimpressed with United Fruit Company's land-grabbing and treatment of the peasants in Guatemala, so he supported democratically elected President Árbenz who had enacted a major land reform program where all uncultivated portions of large land holdings were to be expropriated and redistributed to the landless peasants. The biggest loser here was the United Fruit Company. Long story, short: the CIA got involved, pressured President Árbenz to "take a hike," and shortly thereafter, Guatemala had a well-paid benevolent dictator.

And the United Fruit Company had all its land back.

Che Guevara had this to say: "The last Latin American democracy—that of President Árbenz—failed as a result of the cold premeditated aggression carried out by the United States. Its visible head was Secretary of State John Foster Dulles, a man who, through a rare coincidence, was also a stockholder and attorney for the United Fruit Company."

16

A Difficult Birth

It was the Roaring Twenties, the "Jazz Age," as F. Scott Fitzgerald coined it, women were "Flappers" and, get ready, *they smoked cigarettes, slept around, and chatted openly of sex.* Women's suffrage was out of the closet, morality was in the toilet, rebellion was in the air—and so was Juan Terry Trippe. One particular day that no New Yorker would soon forget was when twenty-three-year-old Juan flew a newsreel cameraman right down the heart of Broadway, twenty feet off the ground, forcing the morning business folk and shoppers to run for their lives. There was going to be hell to pay for buzzing Broadway. Surely young Trippe was headed for a night in the pokey. Or was he? He was arrested, but soon released. There was no law in the early 1920s about flying through the streets of New York City just a few feet over the heads of the terrified, yet after the spectacle, bemused "Broadway strollers."

Again, Juan Terry Trippe couldn't have known it at the time, but forty years later, there would stand in the heart of Manhattan the "largest office building in the world," and it would bear on its lofty sides, in colossal white letters fifteen-feet tall: **PAN AM**. Indeed, an iconic skyscraper that would rise with grand eminence nearly sixty stories higher than he had flown that thrillingly memorable morning back on that sultry summer's day.

By 1924, Long Island Airways business was taking a nosedive as more and more companies catered to the beach crowd and offered service to the Long Island resorts. That, plus the lone Aeromarine down in Honduras had crashed. Some reports had it crashing in the jungle, others into a mountain, either way it killed off that particular lucrative arm of the struggling airline.

Following the demise of Long Island Airways, Trippe founded a number of other companies: Alaskan Air Transport, Buffalo Airways and Eastern Air Transport. With Eastern Air Transport, Trippe went to Washington and lobbied hard to win the very first Air Mail contract between New York and Boston, via Hartford, Connecticut. (Money and security for a fledgling airline came in the form of a government contract.) Problem was, a second, much more well-established company, Colonial Airlines, also was bidding for the contract. Trippe was young, and inexperienced, and the Colonial Airlines board of directors was made up of an impressive group of influential financial-and-political good ol' boys from Massachusetts and Connecticut, including the incumbent Governor of Connecticut.

Knowing Colonial Airlines would get the contract, as his age and lack of experience would rule him out, Trippe, tipped the scales in his favor by adding to his board of directors a few of his former Yale classmates: Percy Rockefeller, William Vanderbilt, Cornelius Vanderbilt ("Sonny") Whitney, and Harvard graduate and WWI combat hero John Hambleton. Hambleton had been awarded the Distinguished Service Cross for his part in aerial combat over France. Plus, Hambleton's father was a well-known and prominent banker, and one of the wealthiest men in Baltimore.

Juan Trippe then cheekily changed the name of his company from *Eastern* Air Transport to *Colonial* Air Transport and, as he was now bringing unimpeachable sources of finance, suggested to the board of directors over at Colonial Airlines that the two companies merge. With the names of some of the most prominent and well-to-do families in America now standing by his side, Juan Trippe suddenly had the attention of the Governor of Connecticut and his hard-drinking army of cronies.

Within days, the companies merged.

Trippe convinced the older stockholders that he alone was the one to run the new company as he already had experience running an airline and could devote his full attention to the enterprise (while they were busy sticking their fingers in a multitude of other juicy pots). Indeed, Juan Trippe was young, but he was poised, self-assured, tall, handsome, and everyone now noticed, and everyone agreed that he should run the company. Trippe even managed to convince the board to keep the name of *his* company: Colonial Air Transport. It didn't hurt his cause that he held mail pilot license number 58, just in case he was needed to stand in for Colonial's modest stable of pilots. And it didn't hurt that he already had experience in the Navy flying at night, you see, in order to guide the planes flying the route after dark, fires had to be lit on the hills surrounding Hartford.

And shortly thereafter, the U.S. Post Office awarded U.S. Air Mail Route contract #1 to Colonial Air Transport. That was the good news.

The not so good news was that Colonial was a paper company and had no planes. But running an airline without airplanes was not such a problem for the indefatigable and unflappable Juan Trippe.

Over the course of the next nine months, Trippe rented airfields that would suit the new route, hired pilots, and negotiated for an *impressive fleet* of aircraft to be delivered—two Ford trimotors and two Fokker trimotors. "The largest order for commercial aircraft ever placed in the United States," he was proud to say, but the curmudgeons on the board of directors (who had no background in aviation) were unimpressed. In their eyes, Trippe was spending money that they just didn't have, or didn't want to part with. The rest of the industry was content with cheaper *single*-engine aircraft.

What was wrong with young Trippe?

About now, on 20 May 1925, some thirteen-hundred miles to the south down in Havana, a new president was assuming the highest office. His name was *el presidente* Gerardo Machado y Morales. Then, just five days later, on 25 May, President Machado ordered the reorganization of the modest Cuban Aviation Corporation.

Simply said, the man like planes.

Flash gently forward to the late autumn of 1925, without notifying his grumpy board of directors, Trippe convinced none other than airplane inventor Anthony Fokker to fly him, and Navy pilot George Pond, down to Havana in the Fokker F-7, the only multi-engine airplane in existence in America. Trippe told Fokker it would be great publicity for his Fokker aircraft.

But Juan Terry Trippe had more up his pinstriped sleeve than promoting the Fokker F-7. Never enamored with his Hispanic name growing up, and certainly not at the coveted six-story brownstone Bovée School (a private boys' academy of social prestige on Fifth Avenue across from the Central Park Zoo), or at his esteemed prep school, the Hill School, in Pottstown, Pennsylvania, and not at all at Ivy League Yale, he was now ready to put "Juan" to good use.

(**AUTHOR'S GOBSMACKED NOTE**: The Bovée School turned out the likes of Efrem Zimbalist, Jr, and Mel Ferrer, and the Hill School has had quite a pedigree of alumni: Academy award film director Oliver Stone, US Senator from Wisconsin William Proxmire, James Baker III Secretary of State, George Patton IV, Alan J. Pakula film director and producer, Lamar and Nelson Bunker Hunt, James Michener author, and, yes, even Donald Trump's two boys, the Donald, Jr. and Eric Trump.)

Trippe, Fokker and Pond landed at Campo Columbia, a military training field on the outskirts of Havana that was also used for Cuba's infant air force, and put on a barnstorming air show the likes of which President Gerardo Machado had never before witnessed.

Machado watched, riveted, as they soared high and buzzed low, flying the Fokker trimotor on all three engines.

Then on *two* engines.

Then, just the *one*.

The Cuban president and the many other Cuban dignitaries present were blown away by the aerial gymnastics and flight capabilities of the plane. Possibly even more impressed that the aircraft had a toilet, as many dwellings in

Havana did not.

And they were impressed with the tall, handsome "Cuban-in-appearance" gentleman named *Juan*.

As many rich American businessmen already had interests in Cuba, such as casinos and racetracks, President Machado proved pleasantly eager and open to supporting American interests on the island.

Especially if he could benefit financially from them.

While Trippe had the president in a good mood, he quickly contacted a Havana lawyer and had him draw up a nifty little document. The document was short, just a few pages, but powerful and cleverly written.

And President Machado gladly signed the document.

Did I say "money exchanged hands"?

I didn't say that.

Did I use the word "bribe"?

I don't remember saying that.

But what I *will* say is that Juan Trippe departed Cuba a few days later with EXCLUSIVE LANDING RIGHTS IN CUBA.

So clever.

He was poised to make his first major step into the Caribbean.

The gateway to South America.

And he now had the key to the gateway.

When Trippe got back to New York, he was dismayed to learn that the board of directors at Colonial Air Transport were less than pleased with his peregrinations. Ready to have an aneurysm, actually. On top of their young operations manager "spending money they didn't have on aircraft they didn't need," he was now flying off to foreign countries when he was supposed to be building an airline back in New York. Trippe countered with the importance of expanding the Air Mail routes down to Miami and Havana.

But the long-in-the-tooth, vision-less board at Colonial were having none of it.

And Juan Trippe was once again without an airline.

Then the hurricane of 1926 tore through Cuba and destroyed most of the hangars and airfield at Havana's Campo Columbia.

But as I've noted before, Juan Trippe was not a man deterred by adversity.

Here's the setup: The Campo Columbia airfield in Havana was being repaired and rebuilt, Juan still held the coveted landing rights, so he decided to go after and win the Key West to Havana U.S. Air Mail contract. He needed a "new" airline company, so, with the aid of his former Yale classmates Bill Rockefeller, Bill Vanderbilt and Sonny Whitney, plus Harvard alum John Hambleton and a few others, together they formed the Aviation Corporation of America, and plopped a whopping $300,000 into start-up seed money. Whitney put up the most money, $49,000 and he was elected chairman, Vanderbilt, Hambleton and Rockefeller were elected president, vice-president and treasurer. Juan Trippe was chosen to be managing director. He was the most experienced in the field of aviation, wasn't he?

Then a hiccup, not a full-blown Icelandic volcanic eruption, just a pesky hiccup, Trippe learned that he had two competitors: one called "Atlantic, Gulf and Caribbean Airways," and the other...

Are you sitting down?

...called "Pan American Airways."

Pan American Airways was just a shell company at the time. No airplanes. No pilots. No iconic blue logo. The Pan American shell company was formed by Major Henry "Hap" Arnold, Major Carl Spaatz, Major Jack Jouett, and Captain John Montgomery. Arnold had been a former intelligence officer, and he knew that Germany was trying to get a stranglehold on the Panama Canal. The Germans already had an airline called SCADTA (*Sociedad Colombo-Alemana de Transportes Aéreos*) based down there in Columbia, in fact Austrian owned, but operating with German planes, German pilots, and German backing. Germany was on the march, the writing was on the wall in *Hochdeutsch*, and Arnold was one of only a handful who was prepared to read it and decipher it.

Arnold envisioned an airline that would extend from Key West, to Havana, and all the way down to Panama.

To give you the short version, Arnold, Spaatz and Jouett exited Pan Am, but retained their names on paper, two fellows by the name of Richard Bevier and George Grant Mason jumped in, and Pan Am was incorporated. Montgomery petitioned the U.S. Post Office to call for bids on the Key West to Havana Air Mail route, and on 16 July, 1927, the contract was awarded to Pan American Airways.

The good news for Juan Trippe was Atlantic, Gulf and Caribbean Airways, and Pan American Airways weren't flying between Key West and Havana.

The better news was that both airlines were still without aircraft.

So let's set the stage: Pan American Airways had the contract to deliver mail to Havana.

Atlantic, Gulf, and Caribbean Airways had access to Wall Street financing.

But Juan Trippe had the exclusive landing rights to Cuba and the ear of Anton "Anthony" Fokker.

Who do you think was going to win here?

Again, the short version: Trippe merged his Aviation Corporation of America with Atlantic, Gulf, and Caribbean Airways. About now, Trippe became aware that there were "terms" to the Pan American contract to deliver mail to Cuba—there was a "deadline"—Pan Am would have to start delivering the mail by the 19th of October, 1927, or lose the U.S. Post Office contract.

Juan Trippe's eyes must have grown as big as coconuts, it was already summer, and the clock was ticking.

Then Trippe went into negotiations with Richard Bevier and his brother at Pan American. The Beviers were hardcore and wouldn't give in. Tick. Tick. Tick. The 19th of October was approaching. And fast. Many concessions were made to Juan Trippe, and he refused each and every one, he held the landing rights, didn't he, and no mail could be delivered if airplanes couldn't land.

As the clock approached the bewitching hour, Juan Trippe simply wore his competition out, never raising his voice or pounding a fist on the table—*his weapon of choice was his intellect* (sound familiar?)—and the brothers Bevier cracked.

The combined forces of Juan Trippe's airline and the Atlantic, Gulf, and Caribbean Airways made Pan American Airways its operating subsidiary. The "new" company retained the Pan American name and Juan Terry Trippe became president and general manager of the combined operations.

Now Trippe needed to get his skates on. He had two Fokker planes that were to be delivered before the 19th, but suddenly there were delays in the delivery. Then heavy rains inundated Key West and turned the island's Meacham Field into a mosquito-infested backwater swamp. The flooding tore into the marl and limestone upon which Key West was built, and sinkholes puckered the airfield. The sinkholes weren't large, but they were deep. One took two tons of rock (that's 400 truckloads worth, to you and me) to fill and it was only a meter wide. As soon as all the holes were filled, runways were finally laid out.

Then the torrential rains came again. Remember, Key West is at 26 degrees latitude, in the middle of the sub-tropics—and hurricane season lasts until November 30th.

And now, to make it all somehow worse, Campo Columbia in Havana was flooding.

Tick. Tick. Tick. Tick.

It was the 17th of October.

One of Trippe's Fokker aircraft was finally ready to roll, but it could only get as far as Miami. Key West's airfield was still under brackish water and it was a no-go zone for landing.

Not in desperation, but thinking on his feet, Trippe flew up to Washington and asked for an extension of the deadline. He was refused.

What to do?

I don't know about you, dear reader, but about now I'm starting to climb the walls laced with mold. But not Juan T. Trippe, for he was the type of guy you wanted on your side when trouble erupted.

And then he had it, an idea that would save his ass, Pan Am, and just possibly the future of aviation.

A floatplane...a *seaplane*.

A floatplane could take off from the placid channel bordering the "flats" at Key West and land in the harbour at Havana. He had flown those floatplanes up at the beaches on Long Island.

Genius.

But where the hell was he going to find a seaplane at the eleventh hour?

17

You Have to Make Your Own Luck

On the 18th of October, Trippe learned that a single-engine Fairchild FC-2, which was configured as a *floatplane*, had just diverted to Miami due to an oil leak. The leak was duly fixed and the seaplane was ready to depart, destination Port-au-Prince, Haiti.

In the opposite direction from Key West.

Trippe struck like a viper and offered to charter the seaplane, but the pilot, Cy Caldwell, a feisty Scot, balked. He was under contract to West Indian Aerial Express based in the Dominican Republic and had to get back to the island. Trippe offered money. Lots of it. Money speaks. Cy Caldwell listened, and he had the seaplane in Key West that very evening, bobbing in the Gulf of Mexico, near the foot of Duval, as the mail train coming down Henry Flagler's Overseas Railroad steamed onto the "Rock."

The following morning, Cy Caldwell skimmed the aquamarine waters off Mallory Dock and lifted his 65-horsepower seaplane *La Niña* into the sun-drenched skies above Key West with seven heavy sacks of Air Mail, containing 30,000 letters! He flew across the Florida Straits and the Gulf Stream at an altitude of one-thousand feet and, sixty-two minutes later, made a smooth landing in Havana's glassy harbour, ninety miles away. There to meet, greet, and complete the delivery was a local Cuban postmaster, who had rowed out to pick up the mail, *on schedule*.

Nothing but net.

Legends made.

An airline born.

Juan Terry Trippe would go on and lead Pan Am from 1927 until 1968, and he would expand Pan Am (from 90 miles to Cuba) into a global network of 81,410 miles, to 86 countries and every continent except for Antarctica. Pan Am could take you almost anywhere in the world you wanted to go, and if trouble erupted in the form of an earthquake or hurricane or armed conflict, Pan Am was there to transport in supplies and evacuate the injured and wounded out.

PART III

18

In-Flight

We were on the verge of flying with the greatest airline the world had ever known...all we needed to do was *survive* In-flight.

In spite of the inherent stress, the four weeks of Training School went by faster than we probably wanted. We enjoyed Training School. We felt secure in Training School. In Training School we didn't have to go climb into a real airplane. But it soon became time for our "In-flight."

Cue distant-and-unnerving primordial screams!

In-flight was a soul-destroying, eye-opening, slap-across-the-face bonus to Training where they actually sent us off across the globe and watched with critical acuity how we fell apart and imploded under fire.

We were all scared of In-flight.

But we got to wear the uniform!

And it almost dissipated the fear.

Almost.

Something one of our trainers had instilled in us during Emergency Week flashed through my brain: "We don't want you to think that when you go out on your In-flight that you're going to have a death, a birth, a fire, a decompression, and then you're going to have to ditch on the way back."

I certainly hoped this wasn't going to be the case.

As fortune would have it, I was paired with Ruth, and we were happy as we could commiserate and be petrified together. We flew a 727 from Miami to Montego Bay through a raging tropical fiesta on what ended up being the first leg of a charter flight. Nobody had told us about charter flights in Training School.

Ruth and I felt totally brain-warped and hopeless. I paid a needed visit to the toilet and couldn't figure out how to flush it. What was I supposed to do, go ask the aft purser how to flush the bog? And I couldn't seem to remember anything I had learned in Training School (where the meals were stored) and then, when I finally did remember exactly what to do, that didn't seem to be the way it was being done "out on the line." All the seasoned flight attendants were doing things patently incompatible with the way we had been taught. When there was a lull in the service and I had a short break, I kindly asked an older colleague working the galley for a coffee, but she offered me orange juice spiked with champagne instead.

I almost fell over right then and there.

And, *no*—thank you very much for asking—I did not accept it.

Other flight attendants had taken up lives of crime. One flight attendant proudly told me she had a complete dinner service for six, crystal wine glasses, china and cutlery, all filched from Pan Am First Class (and sporting the Pan Am logo). Another cabin attendant seemed to be in the blanket and pillow business. If the engines had not been bolted down, I'm sure they would have gone walkabout, as well.

Reality was the rudest of awakenings.

In sunny Montego Bay, Ruth and I had a four-hour layover (because we were foisted off on a new crew who were going up to JFK), so we hired mopeds, went exploring and found what we thought was a secluded beach where we went skinny-dipping until a busload of Germans lay siege to the beach to annex swathes of sand with their beach towels.

The flight to New York was on a packed-to-the-gills 707, filled with senior citizens, and we were pleasantly ahead of schedule. I was thrilled that we would be arriving early and I could soon go somewhere dark and lie down. I was mortified when we started our descent into JFK though, and we hadn't yet cleared the cabin and stowed the meals. We were saved by a quick thinking senior purser who made a clever announcement: "We will be arriving ahead of schedule today and need a bit of help. Any of you lovely ladies ever dreamed about being a stewardess? Well, you can be today! Who wants to give us a hand?" About twenty of the old dears jumped up and, with what I could only describe as Training School smiles, enjoyed every second and we had the cabin cleared, stowed and tables up with time to spare.

Things were certainly different down line, and creativity was a welcomed asset.

We overnighted at the Berkshire Hotel on 52nd and Madison so we could experience a layover. Ruth and I went to the Stage Deli and sipped cream sodas and feasted on scrumptious pastrami sandwiches, and after stuffing our faces, we hustled over to Rockefeller Center, rented skates and went ice skating. I held Ruth's hand and it sent bolts of electricity coursing through my body.

After skating, we walked back to the Berkshire, *not holding hands*. We were shocked to see what looked like colourfully wrapped Christmas or birthday presents resting on some of the brownstone stoops. We would find out later that there was a garbage strike on at the time. Clever New Yorkers, not wanting to be burdened with piles of unwanted trash during the strike, wrapped their garbage up in decorative paper and left them out in the open—to be appropriated.

Back at the hotel, the concierge educated us on the technique of "second acting." I asked Ruth if she wanted to try it out and go see the tail-end of *A Little Night Music* at the Majestic, but she said she had to make a phone call back home to Switzerland and disappeared.

I had a room to myself, so I went back there and watched *Johnny Carson*, with guest host Jerry Lewis.

Lonely.

The next day, after our legal rest, still tired, confused and fearing what lay ahead, we flew off to London working our first 747 with an exceedingly friendly crew. As the aircraft inched down the taxiway, shortly before take-off, the economy purser, with a twinkle in his eye, yelled, "Say, Jon, want to give the emergency demo a try? Good chance to get some practice?"

The demo! I had dreaded this, standing up there in front of all those passengers. Nobody ever paid attention to these demos but for some reason the entire cabin seemed to be staring at me. Even a few of the crew members working First Class had filtered back and taken up positions to observe.

I got through the part about pointing out the exits okay and then the oxygen mask part, but when it came to demonstrate how the life vests worked, things went horribly wrong. Magically, a *live* cartridge had found its way into my life vest and when I "pulled the little red tabs," my vest inflated with an explosive hiss that scared the complete hell out of me, but sent the entire cabin of passengers and crew rolling in the aisles.

At least the blown-up life vest covered my badge which glaringly read: TRAINEE.

And later in the flight, the same friendly crew were inordinately helpful when they showed Ruth how to do the "Ozone Check."

"What's the Ozone Check?" Ruth asked, horrified that she didn't know. "I don't remember that from Training School."

"You take this 'Ozone-ometer,'" explained the same twinkly-eyed purser, holding up an instrument which looked remarkably like a turkey baster. "You have to suck out all the ozone from above the overhead compartments."

"Are you sure about this?" Ruth asked.

"Quite sure, darling," said the purser. "Now you'd better get going. You have a lot of ozone to suck."

I forgot about Ruth until just before the movie started. That's when I went to the aft section of the aircraft and saw Ruth standing on an empty seat still sucking ozone from above the overheads.

Then, just before we began our breakfast service, the New

York based crew made sure I had no trouble with the "Toilet Ph Test" (also not learned in Training School). It went like this: I was passing by one of the aft lavatories, when my favorite purser suddenly sprang out with a paper cup filled with an amount of disgusting yellow liquid. "Jon!" he beckoned. "I've just gathered the 'sample.' Be a good lad and take it to the flight deck and give it to the first officer so he can do the Toilet Ph Test."

"The what?"

"The Toilet Ph Test."

With all eyes on me, and holding the cup with the warm fluid out to the side as if it were a puff-adder, I walked the entire length of the Boeing 747 and up the spiral staircase to the flight deck. I knocked timidly on the cockpit door expecting the worst but was greeted by a remarkably smiley cockpit crew.

"We've been expecting you, Jon. First transatlantic flight, I hear. Well, lookee here, I see you've brought us the sample for the Toilet Ph Test." On this, the first officer put the cup to his lips and downed the entire amount in one gulp.

It wouldn't be until later in the year when Ruth was handing the turkey baster to an unsuspecting trainee and I was handing the paper cup to an aghast newcomer, that I found out the sample for the Toilet Ph Test was just tepid tea.

When we arrived in London on our inaugural trip across the pond, I was looking forward to a layover with Ruth. I had finally plucked up the courage to ask her out on a date. "Hey, Ruth, how about a meal of bubble and squeak in Soho?"

"Love to," she replied enthusiastically. "Meet you in the lobby at noon."

Yay! Finally I was going to be able to reap the benefits of being surrounded by gorgeous women. Now, before you think I was just in it for the sex, that wasn't it at all. Perhaps this would be the start of a great relationship travelling the world?

Sixteen hours later I woke up and it was midnight. I had slept right through our first date.

The next morning, waiting for the crew bus to take us

back to Heathrow to begin our return leg, I spotted Ruth, but before I could utter my profuse apologies she blurted out: "Jon, I'm so sorry I stood you up. All I did was lay my head down on the pillow for a moment, and I didn't wake up until an hour ago. I fell asleep with the TV on. I think I've been shot with an elephant dart."

Strike one for the glamorous, nothing-but-sex airline industry.

The trip back to New York went smoothly: No passengers tried to open the emergency exits mid-flight, we didn't run out of the beef before we reached the last row, and only one child barfed. A good crossing. Just before we started our descent, the First Class purser approached me and seemed just a bit ruffled. "Here, quick, get me your passport. I forgot to log the passport numbers into the, ah, passport log."

"The what?"

"The passport log. Now hurry."

I fetched my passport out of my trusty Pan Am carry-on and handed it over to the purser. She hurried off and grabbed Ruth. Then, just as we were approaching Immigration, the purser sprang out of nowhere. "Ruth! Jon! Here are your passports back. Almost forgot. Sorry!"

Ruth and I thought the rest of the crew were just being polite again when they motioned for us to go through first, but then we found out why. When I handed the Immigration Officer my passport, his face went wraithlike white and the purser and the rest of the crew behind us ignited with laughter.

You see, when the Immigration Officer opened my passport, he saw a picture of Yasser Arafat staring back at him, which was bad, but what was worse, when he opened Ruth's there was an explicitly expressive picture of January's Playmate of the Month—clearly displaying her bountiful credentials. The purser had cut out small pictures and taped them over our regular passport photos.

We shot a look at the Immigration Officer and he actually growled back like he was going to take pleasure in shortening our lives, then the faux storm on his face dissipated, and he, too, roared with laughter, "First time crossing the Atlantic and back as new flight attendants, huh? Well, welcome home. Welcome back to America." (And who said these guys don't have a heart? No, really, who said that?)

19

Drunk with the Spectre of Sex

During Training, we learned that there were four possible bases that successful candidates could be assigned to: New York, Washington, D.C., Miami and London. The coveted bases of Honolulu and San Francisco were far too senior for those fresh out of Training, and it was hinted that "we would all be old and grey by the time they opened."

None of us knew which base we would be assigned, but I wanted London. I did a little checking around and found out that there were only a handful of openings for the London base. Most of us were going to be based in Miami or Washington, D.C. The base in London was new and small and had only just opened the year before. I felt my chances were slim on being awarded it.

I decided to write a heart-felt, most-likely slobbering treatise to the Head of Training, prattling on about my enthusiasm and interest in being based in London. It probably bored her to tears and turned her to drink, but I simply wanted to try something that the others weren't doing: *begging* for the base of my choice.

I don't know if it helped my quest, but just before graduation, I found out I had been granted London, along with Rob Halkides, Wendy Shepherd, Anna-Lise Schwartz and two others: a young lady from Malaysia (who was gagging to do it with Rob), and a young lady from Greece (who didn't know that I existed).

Our class didn't throw a memorable celebratory graduation party, presumably because everyone had repaired to their rooms to pinch themselves, call their mothers, or have an emotional breakdown, so Stan, Rob, Janie, a young lass by the name of Margit, and I decided to celebrate our survival by going on a pub crawl.

After all wasn't that what folk did in London?

We had never ventured anywhere other than our hotel and the Training School facility, so you can imagine how excited we were just to set foot anew and start walking down NW 36th Street in Miami Springs.

Perhaps not so very prudent, present day.

As we strolled along, basking in the glow of life-after-near-meltdown, I noticed that the dress code of my three classmates was in strict contradiction to the Pan Am style that we had just been molded into. Janie was dressed like a slut. Margit like a diva, Rob like a continental dandy. Stan like the British Royal family does when they go to Balmoral in the summer months and dress down. I was wearing shorts and a T-shirt which read: SANTA, I CAN EXPLAIN!

Right off, Janie, who never met a beverage she didn't like, became the unofficial leader of the pack, because she was the first to come up with a cunning game plan: "I will buy a round at the first place we come to that serves alcohol. Yes, I will pay, but *I* get to order whatever I feel like and *you* have to drink it. All of it. *Comprende?*"

Hmmm, I thought, this could really be good crack or turn into embarrassment and disaster.

We set off with a frisson of excitement that comes from accomplishment (not being chucked out of Training School), and the frisson of excitement that is the precursor to alcohol abuse.

We walked for fifteen minutes, but came across no drinking establishments. We were in that no-man's wasteland that is the perimeter of many an international airport—when, say, there aren't strip clubs. We walked for ten more minutes, then, we saw it: a Mexican restaurant. I think it was called the *Pollo Loco*. Or *Chinga el Pollo*. We entered. The A/C was working overtime (in February!) and it was cold enough to hang meat. Or *pollo*. The restaurant was about as dark as a restaurant can be if you don't care to see what you're eating, and I have to say right up front, I've eaten in a few restaurants where I wish I hadn't been able to see the food.

The place was empty and we took seats in a corner in front of a wall mural of a Mexican bullring, where they slaughter God's creatures for sport.

Janie jumped up.

"Where are you going?"

"To order. Gonna be a *sorpresa muy grande.*"

We looked to Stan for the translation.

"Big surprise," he said. "Indeed, quite grand."

Janie ordered from a surly fellow buried under a Mexican sombrero behind the bar, then she returned and pointed at a large, dusty speaker hanging in a dark, dusty corner.

"Hear that? Cuban music. Benny Moré by the sound of it. *Cienfuegos.*"

"How do you know that?"

"Duhhh," Janie said. "Qualified in Spanish, remember?"

Soon, Carmen Miranda's love child cha-chad over to our table and presented us with five drinks in tall, skinny glasses. She shot a flirtatious smile at Stan and disappeared into a black hole.

We studied our drinks. Each had a long green plant sticking out the top.

"What the heck is that," I asked.

"*Cane zuchero,*" Janie said.

"Sugar cane," Stan clarified.

Wow, we were fair impressed. Janie and Stan were not only fluent in Spanish, they knew their exotic drinks.

"*Salud!* To Pan Am! To us! We did it!" Janie squealed, and we sucked eagerly at our beverages like hummingbirds.

"What is it?" Margit asked, holding her drink up and away from her as one might hold a test tube in a lab.

"Mojito," Janie said.

"Oh, aye, mojito," Stan said. "This may be a Mexican restaurant, but it has never seen a Mexican. Everyone in here is well-and-proper Cuban."

INEBRIATE'S NOTE for those of you doing alcohol research: Have you ever had a mojito? Killers, aren't they? They are made, as I mentioned, in a tall glass, then you add enough white rum to kill a *caballo* (or a *pollo*), a dash of lime juice, and a splash of soda water, but you must linger when adding the rum and over pour so the person drinking will get really ripped on just one, and to finish it all off, you stab it with a foot-long piece of sugar cane.

The conversation turned to Training School, as it should. We discussed what scared the shit out of us the most. Watching our weight came in second place just ahead of scrambling eggs to order, in third place. "Emergency Week" was all alone at the top in first place. Emergency Week was harrowing and enervating. There was so much to learn and you had to get it right. That's why Cabin Crew are on the airplane, you know? If you dropped the roast beef on the floor and you chased it down the aisle in First Class with a broom, looking quite the image of the sport of curling, that was a legitimate concern, but nobody was going to die if you yelled: "We'll just use the backup roast beef!" then drop-kicked it back in the galley, gave it a good scrubbing, and served it with a sprig or two of green. But, if the plane went down and you failed to check for fire on the other side of your exit and you opened that door to deploy the emergency slide and allowed the raging inferno in, well, that could NEVER happen. EVER.

About halfway through our mojitos, we discussed the different bases we'd been assigned: Janie and Stan to Miami. Janie was thrilled because Pan Am serviced about a zillion destinations where she could use her Spanish. Plus, she had a thing for Latin men.

For Stan, Latin America would be his oyster to employ his Portuguese and Spanish (and, yes, German), and if he so desired to pop back home to Dallas, it was just a quick hop across the Gulf of Mexico.

Margit was assigned to New York, and this pleased her immensely. She had grown up in a village north of Stockholm, out on the archipelago, and she was drawn to bright lights like a Scandinavian moth. New York City, population 8 million, give or take a few illegal aliens, would suit Margit just fine.

Rob wanted to be based in Seattle or San Francisco, but Seattle was a small base and not accepting anyone. As mentioned, San Francisco was so senior, he would be old and gray or, in his case, really bald before he had a shot there.

Then there was me. Ever since I was little, I wanted to live in London. Perhaps it was *Mary Poppins*, or *Oliver* or *Jack the Ripper* movies, but there was always something olde-worlde and Victorian and very rooftops-of-London that held an allure for me. Plus, London was just across the channel from the continent, and once I was off probation, and I had my flight privileges, I could jet down to go skiing in Zermatt or Kitzbühel.

As mentioned, out of MIA, Stan and Janie would be flying throughout the Caribbean, Central and South America. Out of JFK, Margit would be off to London, Rio, San Paulo, Lagos, Roberts Field, Madrid, Lisbon, Rome. Out of LHR, Rob and I would be hitting Frankfurt, Hamburg, Munich, Paris, Istanbul, Beirut, Karachi, Tehran, New Delhi and Bangkok. Then there would be the charters and that could put anyone of us just about anywhere in the world. There were over 80 cities and 160 hotels worldwide we could turn up at, from Shanghai to Vienna to Sydney to Singapore to Moscow to Tahiti.

We felt we were the luckiest people in the world.

We finished our mojitos, and with a surprising buzz going, waved goodbye to the Cuban staff and stepped out into a muggy, subtropical evening. We turned left and headed farther down NW 36th Street. We stopped and turned as a plane began its take-off roll, we couldn't see it, but we could hear it. The sound was intoxicating as it got louder and louder and finally it took to the sky. In the spectacular flood of lights that is Miami International Airport at night, we could see it was a Pan Am Boeing 707, and perhaps only then did it really hit us that soon we would be flying to those far-off destinations, departing in the middle of the night, arriving in the middle of the night.

Working when others were sleeping, sleeping whenever we had the chance.

The Pan Am 707 was just a speck in the night sky, when Rob broke our reverie and pointed at a structure on the far corner. It was a tumble-down tavern, without a name, just a lonely bulb above a darkened doorway and board-and-batten siding. It looked very much the type of place that was to be avoided.

"My turn!" Rob shouted, and hurried across the street and disappeared inside.

We all looked at each other. Right at that moment, Rob was probably being held at knifepoint, having smoke blown in his face, while he watched a short, somewhat boring sequence of his life (except for Training School) passing before his eyes.

"Let's go in," Margit said.

Margit was Swedish, blonde, blue-eyed, curvaceous in a "just-do-me" sort of way. Going in there with Margit would be like carrying an open flame into an Austrian barn filled with cows.

I glanced at Stan and Janie, they had a look of horror on their faces, Margit was already going in.

We hurried after Margit and just caught up with her as she was opening the door to the cave of inferno. We took baby steps forward. Even darker in here than back at the Mexican restaurant that was Cuban. And no A/C. Hot. Stifling hot. Suffocating hot. It took a moment for our eyes to adjust. I expected to see Rob hanging from his *huevos* just above the bar. But he wasn't hanging above it. He was standing in front of it, talking to the bartender.

"They're having a wee blether," Stan said.

"A what?" I said.

"A chat."

"They're speaking Russian!" Janie said.

We looked around. Everyone in there was sitting at ratty old picnic tables, watching our every move. They all looked like biker types. *Hirsute* Russian biker types. And I'm talking about the women here. The men-folk looked the type you see nowadays on *YouTube* in the compilation of "Bad Russian Drivers," or "Russian Fails." Music tinkled in the background. Melodic. Slow. The balaclava, or was it the balalaika? We took seats at the bar and formed a scrum around Rob. I don't speak Russian, but Rob and the bartender had the kind of body language going that people have when they are house swapping.

And it was clear the bartender had been knocking back the *wodka*.

Finally, Rob turned back to us.

"Did you know this was a Russian bar, Rob?" Janie asked.

"Yeah, there was a black cross drawn above the door. The Magyars do that sort of thing."

"The who?" Margit asked.

"The Magyars. They were Russian nomadic herdsmen. They hung out around the Volga river bend."

"And you could see a black cross in the dark?" Janie asked.

"I've only had one drink."

"A black cross, isn't that how they marked the plague?" I said.

"Black cross, or *red* cross for the plague, laddie," Stan clarified.

"And you know this how?" I said.

"Because I am Mr. Wonderful."

And we all laughed.

I looked at the bartender. I think he was laughing to himself. He slipped off to the other end of the bar to wipe it down, or prepare a poisoned umbrella tip.

"Rob!" I punched him in the shoulder. Do Russians use ricin or mercury on their poisoned umbrella tips?"

"No, that would be the Germans."

"What do the Russians use?"

"Radioactive polonium. Hard to trace."

"No pun," Stan said.

Rob yelled across to Janie. "Hey, Janie, what would your favorite layover be?"

"What do you mean?"

"Once we get out on the line. What would make a perfect layover?"

Janie thought for a moment. "Meet *señor* Right. Shag him. Spend my life in a warm country spending *señor* Right's money."

"Margit?"

Margit thought for a moment. "A charter to Stockholm. My parents get to see me in my uniform."

"That's it? No sex?"

"Yes, Rob, that's it. Everything doesn't have to be about sex."

"You're Swedish. Didn't you sort of invent it all?"

"That would be the Danes."

Rob let this sink in for a while, then turned to me: "Jon?"

I thought for a moment. "Great cockpit crew. Great cabin crew. We are in Beirut and we all go to dinner together."

"That's it? No sex?"

"No, but I get to meet someone who loves languages and travel."

"What about the sex?"

"I've only just met her. Give it some time."

Rob turned to Stan. "And for you, Stanford?"

"Couple of nights in Edinburgh. During Hogmanay. Down a wee dram or three. Get to wear my kilt."

"You own a kilt?" Janie said.

Janie, Janie, Janie…I am descended from Clan Fraser. It's not that I own a kilt that's unusual, it's that I own a proper pair of trousers."

This made perfect sense to us. We all said: "Rob?"

Rob thought for a moment. "I'm in Russia. I meet the perfect woman, but she's married. We meet clandestinely and make love, but she must return to her husband. It's winter. She's cut off by snow…"

"Wait! Wait! Wait!" Stan said, "That's *Doctor Zhivago*!"

The bartender grunted. He was back. He placed five glass jars on the transom in front of us. Inside each was an enormous amount of dangerous-looking liquid. It was dangerous-looking because it was clear.

"What the hell is it?" Janie asked.

"It's called *Sputnik!*" Rob said.

"Sputnik!" I blurted out, albeit in that loud, ebullient way one does when alcohol is beginning its insidious path of destruction.

And on that, the bartender, who had eyebrows that Leonid Brezhnev would have been proud to call his own, lit each of the drinks with his Bic lighter and WHOOSH there was a moderately impressive exo-thermic reaction.

"FIRE!" Stan bleated, as we had done frequently during Emergency Week.

"*Nastrovia!*" Rob said calmly. "Test it with your tongue. It's an elixir, but a sinister one. It will burn a hole all the way down to your backside."

"You serious?"

"*Da!*"

We tested with flicking tongues, Louie and the lizards sitting at the bar. We lapped at our drinks in a choreographed fashion, and the bartender's face swept with a wonderful smile. Sort of like a flash fire.

I looked around at all the other patrons/felons and they weren't staring at us anymore.

The bartender disappeared for a moment, then returned with a tray topped with small plates, bearing what looked to be victuals harvested from road kill.

"*Zakuska!*" he said.

We turned to Rob.

"Appetizers. We need to eat something after we drink or we'll topple over."

"Think I'm already on my way," I said.

"That because of the Sputnik."

"Huh?"

"It's the *wodka* we're drinking."

"How do you know this *wodka* is Sputnik?"

"Because it will put you in orbit."

"Gag me!" Janie said.

"Yer speakin' oot yer arse, nu," Stan said in his best Glaswegian.

Rob carried on. "If you've lost all sensation below the waist, it's because of the Sputnik. It's 80 proof, that's forty percent. If it's above 80 proof, it's really no longer vodka."

"And you know all this because…?"

"He-lo-o!" Rob sang. "Qualified in Russian. Lived in Moscow for a while. Destroyed some brain cells in the local *ryumochnaya*…"

We studied the seemingly tasty, albeit, mystery *zakuska*, the bartender had made up for us. Rob sensed our concern, then launched into a bout of clarification.

"*Zakuska* essentially are cold dishes. It could also be yesterday's leftovers. It can be salted sturgeon, smoked ham, caviar, pickled mushrooms, salted salmon, salted just about any fish really."

Stan said: "You are a fountain of knowledge, laddie!"

"You've heard nothing yet. When I would go to a Russian party, which seemed pretty much the only thing I did over there, we would sit around and knock back *wodka* and hit the *zakuska*, big time. This would go on for a couple of hours. Hard on the head the next day, but a great way to learn colloquial Russian." Rob slipped into deep thought for a moment: "No wonder no one in Russia gives a shit about the cold."

Margit chimed in: "In Sweden we used vodka to disinfect wounds."

"Sacrilege! I'd rather lose a limb," Rob said.

"We use it to clean diesel engines, as well," Margit said.

"You're killing me!" Rob moaned.

Rob turned to the bartender. The bartender was watching us like a parent watches a small child eat. He seemed to be glowing. Rob spoke to him in Russian again.

"What did you say?"

"I asked him how long he's been in Miami."

"And?"

"Nearly 35 years. Since they built the airport." Rob added: "Did you know that when Miami was Pan Am's main hub, they had their own airfield called Pan American Field? Pan Am eventually sold the airfield and it became present day Miami International Airport. Right over there across the street."

"You are indeed a fountain of knowledge," Janie said.

"*Na Zdorovie!*" And we lapped our drinks. Yikes! It was like drinking industrial strength acetone.

Rob started to take his trousers off.

Janie was delighted: "You're dropping trou!"

But Margit was mortified. "Rob! What are you doing?"

"Just undoing my belt," Rob said. "Everything doesn't have to be about sex, you know."

And we all laughed.

Rob pulled his belt through the loops on his trousers and turned the belt over so we could see. It had a long zipper. Rob unzipped the belt and pulled out a twenty dollar bill. "Cool, huh, I bought it in case we ever get to go to Lagos. Or Rio."

Rob paid, and the bartender mumbled something back.

"Now what did he say?"

"He said he gave us a Pan Am discount!"

"How did he know we were Pan Am?"

Rob asked the bartender. The bartender responded, then smiled at all of us.

"He said he heard us say Pan Am, that, plus it was written all over our faces."

"Did he just grunt again?"

"No, that was Russian this time. He wished us good luck."

We slalomed out of the no-name tavern, murmuring "*Spasibo*," and aimed for our next port of call. We hoped we would find another bar before we hit Miami Beach—or Bimini.

As we walked, I was overcome by a blast of joy I had never felt before. I was in my element. Among folk of similar soon-to-be worldly wealth who revelled in travel and languages. It was overwhelmingly exciting.

Margit wanted to go next, and you can well imagine her supreme disappointment when we came to a Howard Johnson's.

"This is no good," Margit said.

"It serves alcohol," Janie said. "We have to go in. Those are the rules."

So we did. And just so you know, when you've just come from the Russian equivalent of *Cheers* ("where everybody knows your plane"), and you are fantasizing about distant sun-drenched beaches, quaint cobblestoned Old Towns, Scottish castles, and bustling fragrantly heady souks, Howard Johnson's really slaps you rudely across the face and smashes you back to reality.

We sat at a red table in a red corner and Margit sulked. She wanted something exotic and with perhaps just the *hint* of danger. The only hint that Howard Johnson's had, was a hint of kitsch.

Then Margit's blonde cherubic face lit up and she bolted and corralled a passing waitress. Soon, she returned, and repeated the theme of the evening: "I ordered it. I paid for it. You've got to drink it."

"No problem there!" Janie squealed.

"Too right, hen!" Stan slurred.

We all looked at each other. It was only Howard Johnson's, how exotic could this get? This is when two waitresses in matching red candy-stripes walked up holding two pitchers of beer each. Just like the Hofbräuhaus in Munich, but without the fetching, plunging dirndls.

"A pitcher of beer each?" Janie said. She was impressed.

"Let me tell you something about Sweden and drinking alcohol," Margit began. "We are professionals, perhaps not quite as major league as the Icelanders, but we pride ourselves in our ability to get fall-down drunk in public..."

"Commendable," Stan said.

"Does Sweden's drinking problem have anything to do with Sweden's uncommonly high rate of suicide?" Rob asked.

"No," Margit said, quite frankly. "That has to do with the

summer."

"The summer?"

"Yes, it comes in May and lasts but a few days."

We all nodded our complete understanding.

"*Skol!*" Margot intoned, and we dived in to our pitchers like five dehydrated Swedes.

Just so you know, dear reader, if you down a mojito, followed by *wodka* and start chasing it with a frothy pitcher of Budweiser, you feel exceedingly happy. As long as you don't have to do something rash, such as attempting formal conversation or making swift decisions.

"Sweden," Margit began, "is part of the vodka belt. I think we invented binge drinking. If not us, for sure the Brits. Everyone thinks the Swedes are big drunks, and I tell you why. It costs a fortune to buy alcoholic beverage in Sweden. Sale of alcohol is strictly government controlled. If you want to buy one lonely bottle of beer that is stronger than snake piss, you can't in a supermarket. Must buy from government store. Long queue to stand in. Government store called *systembolaget*. We have 400 state-run liquor stores in Sweden. *Skol.*"

And we drank.

"If you go to nightclub, you have to take loan against house to be able to afford. At Midsummer, it stay light almost all night. We don't sleep much. We have midnight sun. We have crayfish parties—reason to drink—reason to get shit-faced. At Christmas we take holiday seriously, and with respect as one should, so only get hammered. But alcohol still dear, so, when we go on holiday, abroad, booze for us is very, very cheap and we get wasted. That's why everyone thinks Swedes are big drunks."

"I'll drink to that," Rob said.

"*Skol!*" Margit said.

"*Slàinte!*" Stan said.

And we drank.

And we talked about Pan Am.

"What unnerved you the most about Training School, sire?" Stan asked.

"Diane Roberts," I said. "She was so attractive and so intelligent and so humorous…"

"Women like that intimidate you?" Janie said.

"This one did."

Janie wagged a finger sideways at me and said as teenagers do to each other: "Jon likes Diane…Jon likes Diane…"

"*Prost!*" I said.

And we drank.

"What scared you, Janie?" I asked.

"The movie of the plane ditching. That freaked me out. What do we do if something really happens?"

We all went quiet for a long time. What if something *did* happen? Would we survive? Would we be strong? A leader? In charge? Could we crawl along the floor of a burning aircraft, trying to keep low to avoid suffocating smoke and toxic fumes? Could we evacuate people out of a burning aircraft?

Out an over-wing exit?

Out a hole in the fuselage?

Shiver.

Little did any of us know it at the time, but that's exactly what one of our dear classmates was going to have to do. And it wasn't going to be pretty. Hundreds would die. Incinerated in an inferno the likes of which the aviation industry had never before witnessed.

"*Skol*," someone said, ripping us from our thoughts, and we downed our pitchers of beer and wobbled out of a Howard Johnson's that is no longer there.

We stumbled on farther down NW 36th Street, to the east. Five drunk skunks, arm in arm, like sailors on shore leave. We had been through a tiny corner of hell called Training, and we had, out of safety in numbers, formed a glorious bond.

We walked on for about twenty minutes and saw nothing that resembled an oasis. We stopped.

"Let's go back," I said. "I don't think there are any other bars this side of Biscayne Bay. But it's still my shout and I get to choose one of the three places we've already visited."

"Not in the rule book," Janie said, "but I will accept it as 'needed hydration', therefore a life-saving amendment."

When we got to the Howard Johnson's, I feigned as if I were going in, then stopped. Everyone laughed and blew out their cheeks.

We stumbled on: Five sailors no longer on shore leave, rather now on a ship, rolling, pitching and yawing. When we reached the no-name, hang-you-by-the-privates' Russian bar, I did the same thing. I faked as if I were going in.

Then I went in.

"Yesss!" Rob said, making a fist and jerking it downward.

The Russian bar was even darker than the last time, if that was possible in the scope of physics. As before, everyone watched us cross to the bar. We took seats on the same stools we had sat on before.

"They seem much higher now," Stan noted.

The music was different. Dirge-like. The bartender's face was even more flushed (much like ours), and he had a smile on his face as he stood there, fists on hips, like Yul Brynner in the *King and I*. Then he belted something out in Russian.

We all turned to Rob.

"He said 'Your mother looks like a ferret.'"

Stan piped up. "Rob, focus! I don't *parliamo* Russian, but I'm quite sure he wouldn't say that."

"You're right. Just messing with you. He said: 'Welcome back, and your mother looks like a ferret.'"

"Rob!"

"Okay, he asked what we wanted to drink."

Everyone turned to me now.

"What are you going to do?" Janie asked. "You don't speak Russian."

"The man has lived in Miami for 35 years. His English is probably better than mine, and the majority of residents of Greater Miami. Plus, I only need to know one word in Russian."

"What's the one word?"

"Top secret," I slurred.

"That's two words," Stan slurred.

"No, I mean, I can't tell you the one word as it's extremely *top secret*."

"It better be good," Janie said.

"Oh, but it will."

I leaned forward in a sort of inebriated, conspiratorial manner to the bartender. He leaned forward, the drunk co-conspirator. And I spoke my one word. Immediately the bartender threw his arms in the air in a "No, not that!" manner, crossed himself and disappeared in the shadows behind a poster of the Kremlin.

Everyone shot me a look.

And we waited.

The bartender finally appeared out of his laboratory, balancing a small round tray on one hand. He placed the tray in front of us. On it were five shot glasses.

"That's it?" Stan barked. "Just five shots?"

The bartender rolled his eyes and crossed himself again.

"What is it?" Margit asked.

"It's Slivovitz," I said.

Stan let go with a silent scream, then asked: "How do you know about Slivovitz?"

"It was my undoing in Austria once."

"Geez," Rob said. "Slivovitz isn't cigars-and-fireplace brandy enjoyed by the gentry out in the *dachas*. I may have to be a piker and drop out."

"No can do," Janie hissed. "One for all, and all for getting legless. It can't be that bad. What is it, Jon?"

"It's simply plum brandy, but it's the way it's distilled. The good stuff, which is in fact the bad stuff, is made by leaving the pits in. The pits contain amygdalin. It's a precursor to cyanide."

"Well, shit on a wall!" Stan said.

"An appropriate response," I replied. "Slivovitz is produced all over Eastern Europe. The Serbs love it, as do the Czechs and Poles. Its origin is a bit of a mystery as Russia invaded Poland so many times, it's not known if it was the Poles or the Russians who invented it…"

The bartender grunted. We look to Rob for succor.

"*Russian*," he said. "And I'm not about to argue with him."

The bartender disappeared for a moment again, and soon returned with five small beers. He said something to Rob. Rob listened intently, then turned toward us. "He says for us to be sure to drink the entire beer afterwards or we will self-immolate."

"You know the word for 'self-immolate' in Russian, laddie?" Stan asked, gobsmacked.

"No, he actually said 'Die a horrible fiery death'."

"Did he really say that?"

'No."

"So are we going to do this?" Janie said.

"We have to throw it right down," I began.

"All of it?"

"Yes, *all* of it. Then you have to exhale like hell or you will have one more orifice than you came with. Believe me when I say this."

With quivering hands, Stan, Janie, Margit and Rob reached out for their shots of Slivovitz. The bartender slid our five small beers within striking distance. I held up my shot. The others held up theirs. *Prost!*" I said.

"*Salud!*" Janie said.

"*Skol!*" Margit said.

"*Slàinte!*" Stan said.

"Oh, shit!" Rob said.

And we threw our shots of Slivovitz down.

"FIRE!" Stan yelled.

Margit didn't say anything, just coughed a lung out because she forgot to exhale.

"Drink your beers!" I said. "Hurry!"

And we drank.

And Margit coughed.

"That's vile!" Stan hissed. "It's like drinking petrol!"

"Worse!" Margit coughed.

We hung out at the no-name Russian bar for a while.

"I have no feeling below the waist," Stan said.

"I can't feel my tongue," Janie said.

Rob was the first to attempt formal speech: "Have you flown much, Janie?"

"Since I was little. Mostly down to Cabo San Lucas, or over to Cozumel."

"Jon?"

"Mostly Europe. I dreamt of the Alps when I was a boy."

"You dreamt of buxom *Fräuleins* serving golden steins of beer, you just thought it was the Alps," Janie said.

"Ha. Ha."

"Stan?"

"To Scotland every time I got the opportunity."

Rob looked at Margit, who was still holding her throat. "Margit?"

"I never flew until I came to Training School."

"Why?"

"I was afraid of flying…"

My eyes were now nothing but slits and I tried to focus in on Margit.

"Well," I began, "that would beg the question what are you doing working for an airline?"

"I love to travel. Just hadn't done any by air."

"Let me get this straight," Rob said. "You have never flown before now, and you're afraid of flying?"

"Yes."

"Och! How did you get from Sweden to Miami?" Stan asked.

"I drank."

"How did you get through In-flight, don't tell me you drank?"

"I wasn't quite as afraid, because I understood so much more about airplanes and flying."

"Knowledge is power," Stan said. Then: "What about you, Rob?"

"L.A. to Moscow. As often as I could. While I was at UCLA, and after I graduated."

"A long trip," Janie said.

"That wasn't the problem," Rob said. "I'm a lousy packer."

"What?"

"I always pack too much and take things I don't need…"

"Like what?"

"A travel iron."

"All hotels have those."

"I realize that, but what if one doesn't, or it's not working, or the setting is too hot and it's stuck?"

"Rob!" Stan hissed, "About now I would say 'Check, please!' but Jon-Boy is buying. What else do you take that you don't need?"

"Two face cloths…"

"TWO!"

"One for shampooing my moustache, and the other for washing the bottom of my feet."

We were all stunned, and it was no longer from the Slivovitz.

"You wash the bottom of your feet?" Margit said.

"You shampoo your moustache?" Stan said.

"What?" Rob said, with an innocent look on his face.

* * *

Stan had not had his turn to order and perpetuate the destruction of grey matter, so when we got back to the hotel, we took seats over in the corner *by the scale* and he ordered us five wee drams of scotch (which were not so wee).

We decided to have one for the yellow brick. Then another. And another.

"This is just how it will be when we're out on the line," Janie mused.

"No one would do that, would they?" Stan slurred. "Drink themselves into a stupor and then fly the next day…"

20

Graduation, and Off to London

Diane Roberts pinned on my wings at Graduation, and my heart was beating so loudly I was afraid she could hear it.

Then we had our class photo taken. A proper tableau of beaming smiles and lots of teeth.

One by one, we shipped out to our respective bases and our new homes. Rob, Wendy Shepherd, the young lady from Malaysia, the damsel from Greece, and I, flew out to Montego Bay, this time on a 707. It was a full load, and we all did our best to help the *real* cabin attendants with their duties. We got in the way a lot, and gave kosher meals to nuns and the beef to the vegetarians, but no one seemed to mind. The crew was very patient and didn't play any practical jokes on us. Just before landing at Sangster International, the captain asked if I wanted to sit in the cockpit for landing. I wanted to say that we were told in Training School that this was strictly against FAA rules, but then he was the captain, wasn't he, and I wasn't about to refuse an offer from…God.

Why did he ask me and not the others? Presumably he asked me, because I kept finding reasons to take him, the first officer and flight engineer coffee, so I could see what the cockpit of a 707 looked like.

If you ever get a chance to sit illegally in the cockpit, landing in Montego Bay, I highly recommend it. But be forewarned, the runway in Montego Bay does not look so very big from way up there in the observer's seat of a 707. Actually, now that I say that, Jamaica doesn't look so big from up there. And on final, I was shocked to see how high we were in relation to how close we still were to the airport. All cabin attendants should be able to do a few take-offs and landings in the cockpit, get the opportunity to listen to the tower, watch in awe how focused the cockpit crew are. Makes for a bit more understanding when you're working the back of the bus.

The captain skillfully dropped the 707 down and made what I thought was an absolutely beautiful landing. I thanked the captain and, after ushering all the passengers out, we deplaned.

We had a few hours before the 2nd leg of our journey to New York, so Rob, the Malaysian girl, who seemed to be increasingly infatuated with Rob (did she know about his clean feet?), Wendy Shepherd, the Greek girl, and I, grabbed a taxi and had him take us to the nearest beach. The beach was not far from what is now Sandals, and we all changed in the bushes and went swimming in the Tanqueray-clear sea.

Wendy had a camera, so we snapped lots of photos to send back to our parents.

Our flight to JFK was with a new crew on a chocka 707. All the jump seats were taken, so the captain asked me if I wanted to sit in the cockpit on take-off. Am I lucky, or what? Yes, lucky until we started our roll-out and I saw the mountain at the end of the runway with the wreckage of a small commuter plane strewn all over it. Might I just mention, if you ever get the chance to sit in the cockpit of a jet taking off from Montego Bay, perhaps give it a miss. Unless you're a pilot of course, as you will have nerves of steel and your testicles won't shrivel and try to hide indoors as mine did. If you are a female pilot reading this, keep the "nerves of steel" part, and scratch the testicles. I mean, scratch the part about the testicles.

On our flight to JFK, we endeavoured to help the *real* crew, only to find out, once again, that how things were taught to us in Training School was not one-hundred percent how it was done in the wild blue yonder. Perhaps about fifty-one percent, I'm guessing.

The New York based crew was kind and helpful and made sure that each of us did the announcements in *all* of our languages. Between the five of us, that made English, German, Spanish, Italian, French, Standard Malay, Greek, Russian and Serbian. It wasn't until the end of the flight when the senior purser gave credit to the languages being spoken by "Our five trainees who were on the way to their London base," did we realize that perhaps we had been, well, *had*. Nevertheless, everyone applauded, and only a few laughed, and even though we had been used for amusement, we were somewhat chuffed: Doing the announcements in a foreign language or two when you are a new flight attendant is daunting, but at least—taken advantage or not—we had got our feet wet and it wasn't so terrifying the next time. Plus, one elderly lady on the way back home to New York was Russian by birth and she found Rob's Russian "quite a pleasant surprise and one of the reasons she loved flying Pan Am."

We arrived at a wintery JFK on time and, *no*, I did not get to sit in the cockpit for landing.

My memory fails me here. Can't remember what we did for a few hours at JFK in the stunning and high-tech Pan Am Worldport terminal, probably spent the time pinching ourselves again on account of our dream coming true, and running about the concourse with our hands in the air.

Or perhaps we were directed to the crew desk in OPS, or the crew lounge, and we sat there with our mouths hanging open and our tongues lolling, admiring all the smart-looking uniformed Pan Am cockpit and crew.

You can see that I'm struggling with recall here.

Eventually, we were herded into a 747 for our flight to London. We boarded with the crew and almost felt like crew ourselves. Almost. We had all been on a 747 before, but never an *empty* one. And aren't they big? And wide? And long? The In-Flight Director's name was Muffy Harmar, and she assigned me to First Class, and the others to economy. I thought I was going to keel over having to serve First Class passengers. I felt a bit of a fraud, but Muffy Harmar must have read the horror on my face and became very protective. "Just stick with the others," she said. "And observe. You can help us clear after the dinner service."

Muffy studied me for a moment, then said: "There's no room for you on a jump seat, and we're full upfront. Want to sit in the cockpit for take-off?"

I *know*, I couldn't believe it either, taking off in the cockpit of a 747, at night, on our way to London. I was absolutely over the moon.

Having said that, have you ever timed how long you have to taxi at JFK on a busy night? It's long. We taxied so long, I thought that perhaps there was a land-bridge to London that I didn't know about. And sitting in the cockpit of a Pan Am Clipper 747, at night, over three stories off the ground, seeing the shimmering lights of towering skyscrapers off in the distance, well, that was an experience I would not soon forget.

The captain kindly gave me the headset for the observer's seat and I got to listen to all the chatter, and I must say it was uniquely rewarding.

When the dinner service in First Class was over and the passengers were settling down to a brandy, *a smoke*, sleep or the movie, I slipped into the back to see how Rob and Wendy were doing.

"This is a London-based crew," Wendy told me. "These are the people we will be working with."

Well, I was thrilled. I couldn't wait to have the opportunity to fly with this crew again, especially Muffy Harmar.

Flying from New York to London in the winter time, through the night, became one of my favorite things. There's still not a hint of light in the sky as you pierce Irish airspace, cross the Irish Sea, soar high above the Cornish coast and descend lower and lower on approach to Heathrow. Down below, lights from cottages and farms twinkle sleepily back, and the orange glow of the sodium street lights add a strange warmness. I never tired of that back then, and even today, I never tire of it. While the airplane is bathed in a symphony of deviated-septum snores, I stare out the window and mumble to myself: "That's Ireland down there, and that's England: Cornwall, Devon Dorset, Berkshire and home."

We landed at Heathrow on time, deplaned with the rest of the crew, then as they went to their families, lovers or commuter apartments, we were whisked by a Pan Am crew bus to an airport hotel, just beyond the end of civilization.

And it was still dark.

We were exhausted from jet-lag, stress and anticipation, and our feet were killing us. We had flown from Miami to Jamaica, changed planes, Jamaica to New York, changed planes, then through the night to London.

"I'm going to shower," Rob said. "I feel like shit."

Rob showered. Probably washed his feet. When he came out I asked him: "Feel any better?"

"Wet and feel like shit."

I showered. When I came out, Rob had the black-out curtains closed and he was already in bed. "Are you shattered?"

"I could sleep for a week."

I pulled the covers back on my bed and got in. Even though it was only 8.30a.m., I said: "Goodnight, Rob."

"'Night…"

I was just about to drift off, when I heard a knock at the door. "Pssst, Rob, someone's at the door!"

"I heard it. Let's ignore it."

"Goodnight."

"'Night."

Knock. Knock.

We didn't budge.

KNOCK. KNOCK. Louder now.

"For crissakes!" Rob moaned. "All I want to do is sleep and I can't! I'm going to kill whoever is out there!"

Rob sprang up, charged the door and threw it open.

"Who is it?" I whispered.

But there was no response. In the dim lighting of the hall, I could just make out the Malaysian girl from our Training class leading Rob away by the hand. Then, someone shut the door and crawled in bed with me. She was completely naked, and she said these words to me: *"Den boroúsa na koimithó."*

I didn't know what the young lady had just said, but I knew what language it was.

Greek.

My big fat Greek layover.

21

My First Flight!

I woke up and it was dark out. I had no idea what time it was. Where I was. What country I was in. But one thing I did know was that when I rolled over, Rob would be sawing wood in the other bed and all that "had happened" would have just been an unrequited wishful fantasy which had been brought on by sleep deprivation and, well, lack of getting laid that millennium.

I rolled over. No Rob. I rolled the other way, and there she was—Miss Rhodes, a sexually parched siren with a camel's thirst.

Crikey!

Is *this* what it was going to be like working for the airline? Gorgeous instructors at Training School and demoiselles slipping into my bed to seek warm, albeit rabid, solace? I looked over at Miss Rhodes again and a pair of large brown spaniel eyes were staring back at me.

"*Páli?*" she said in sultry Greek.

As before, I had no idea what she said, and I was about to ask her to translate, when she rolled over onto her stomach. I was contemplating my next move and trying to form a map of Greece in my mind, when the phone rang.

I leaned over and picked up the receiver. "Hello."

"Rob Halkides?" came a British accent.

"No, he's not here right now. Can I take a message?"

"Who's this?"

I identified myself, then asked: "But who are you?"

"This is Graham in Scheduling. You'll do."

"I'll do what?"

"I have a flight for you. Be here at 6am."

"You have a flight for me?"

I looked over at Miss Rhodes, she was climbing out of the bed and wrapping a towel around her nakedness. "I'd better get back upstairs, they'll be calling me next."

And she was out the door.

"What time is it, Graham?"

"It's almost four…"

"Which four?"

"What do you mean?"

"Four *a.m.* or four *p.m.*?"

"Four a.m. Got to go."

CLICK. Graham rang off.

"Where am I going?" I said to the receiver. "It's probably just a Paris turnaround, I'll be back in time to meet Miss Rhodes for seconds."

"Breakfield!!!"

"Graham? Are you still there?"

"Put the phone down!"

I hung up, quickly showered, shaved in the shower, and I was wired from impending adventure. I didn't pack a suitcase as I wouldn't be gone long, just took my flight bag and my thick, heavy, hernia-inducing manual.

I caught the shuttle bus to the airport. An exceedingly chatty chap drove me over to Terminal 3. I admired him for being so pleasant after working through the night.

I nervously entered the Pan Am lounge which was adjacent to Scheduling. I went and introduced myself to Graham. Graham was harried, but super friendly.

"Jon! Thanks for coming!"

"I'm excited to be going to Paris, even if it's just there and right back." (The Paris turnaround was less than an hour over and less than an hour back. The London base picked up the back end of the LA nonstop to London continuation-to-Paris flight. Some of the London-based crew who were French, or other nationalities who wanted to improve their French, used the flight as a sort of a taxi service. Many F/As who were married, would bid for schedules loaded with Paris turnarounds so they could be home later in the day to hang out with hubbies and mollycoddle carpet crawlers.)

"Oh, but you're not doing a Paris turnaround," Graham said. "You're going to Delhi. Seven-day trip."

"Me? I'm going to Delhi?"

"That you are. Let me show you where your mailbox is."

Delhi! Wow and yikes. *Wow* because it meant laying over in Beirut on the way out and the way back...and *yikes* because I didn't have a change of underwear or uniform shirts. That's when I remembered something that had been pounded into our muddled brains in Training School: "Always be prepared for a change of plans, flights, delays, scheduling."

Gulp.

I went to the briefing room and found that I was the second one there. The first one there was the IFD, the In-flight Director. Her name was Corolla. And she was smiling broadly at me. The London base was small and she knew that this was my first flight.

We introduced ourselves and Corolla had me sign in, picking the station on the 747 where I wanted to work.

"You're not going to assign it to me?"

"No."

"Doesn't it go by seniority?"

"Paul Newman's on the flight. All the gals will fight for the front. Take anywhere in the back. It will be safe back there."

So I signed in—GALLEY.

What the hell was I doing opting for economy galley on my first flight? It seemed less threatening. I wouldn't have to deal with real live passengers.

What could possibly go wrong?

One by one other cabin attendants began to filter in. All female. When it was all over, we were a cabin crew of 18, just me and 17 well-groomed, multi-lingual, well-travelled, well-crafted, cultured, attractive members of the opposite sex. I thought I would faint.

BUG-EYED NOTE: Can you imagine the luxury of eighteen cabin crew on a 747 today?

Eventually, the captain came in and gave us the flight times, conditions and other pertinent information. We would be flying one hour to Frankfurt, picking up/dropping off passengers, then two hours to Istanbul, same story, then two-and-a-half hours to Beirut and laying over.

To say I was excited does not begin to capture the moment. I was absolutely floating on air. Here it was my very first flight, and I was working for Pan Am, based in London, flying to nearly the ends of the earth.

* * *

On our flight to Beirut, I was not only the lone male flight attendant, I was the only American (which secretly I found exotic, not me being American, I mean to say on account of all the others being a cross-section of the world). When the London base had opened the previous year, many foreign-born cabin attendants who had been based around Pan Am's system transferred to London to be closer to family, friends and home in the UK and down on the continent. This accounted for our cabin crew consisting of three ladies from England, one from Ireland, one from Finland, one from Scotland, and the rest from Sweden, Denmark, France, Italy, Germany, Spain, Norway…and one from Australia who was married to an English stock broker chap. And they were all older and fairly senior.

And they all looked after me.

The lone dog in the pound that nobody wanted.

Until now.

* * *

Working the galley for the first time was daunting, stressful, but safe, away from judgmental eyes of the paying passengers. It was a very light load and in retrospect that's probably why Corolla didn't flinch when I signed up for the galley.

All the other flight attendants gave me useful tips and pointers on how to fire up the quirky, mercurial ovens and what I should do if I dropped the bread rolls on the galley floor. *Gather them back up, brush them off, reheat, and serve.*

I didn't mention that this was my first time working galley, but everyone knew. I've always been a fairly organized person and organization is what economy galley is all about.

Having said that, there was the odd moment of terror.

Everything was going swimmingly until we were doing the meal service out of Istanbul. We were serving coq-au-vin and I thought I was being, well, extremely organized when I filled two coffee pots with the glutinous gravy, so I could quickly and efficiently give the coq-au-vin a good dousing as they came out of the ovens. It wasn't until the end of the service, when we were serving coffee, did I realize that one of the stewardesses had inadvertently grabbed a pot with the gravy instead of coffee. She came back into the galley with the most stunned expression on her face when she realized what she had done. "I served a Turkish family gravy instead of coffee!"

"Were they upset?" I asked, mortified.

"No, they wanted seconds!"

And near the end of the service, I was eagerly shown how to "magically make a new dinner materialize out of thin air" when one of the gals working the aft section tripped and dumped that last beef entrée in the aisle. Quickly, she rounded up the bits and pieces, salad, dessert, cutlery, napkin, salt and pepper, and creamer which had rolled under the four seats in the middle. Then she stuck just her outstretched arm in the galley, holding the offending, and now splattered tray in front of me: "Here, Jon," she said, bellowing so everyone who had witnessed the unfortunate event could hear, "Take this, will you, and give me a fresh dinner!"

I watched oh so impressed as three senior cabin crew rushed to our aide and, harvesting bits and pieces from trays which had already been returned, built a "fresh" tray. All I had to do was wipe up some spillage off the tray, pick some lint off the old beef and give it a good splash with the ever popular coq-au-vin gravy.

"Here we go!" beamed the flight attendant, returning to the cabin, "You don't get this kind of service on British Airways!"

* * *

Flying into Beirut was quite the eye-opener. We came in parallel to the beach and set down right next to the sparkling Mediterranean. We were so close to the lapping waves, I could have walked to the water and dipped my toes in.

We swept through Customs and Immigration and this was when I first realized that Pan Am crew back then were treated like something between rock stars and royalty. The airport was absolutely abuzz with curious gawkers, intrigued by the likes of us who represented a world away. And perhaps a coveted rung or two higher up the ladder.

On the way into Beirut on the crew bus, one of the French speaking cabin attendants asked the bus driver if he could take the beach road as it was more picturesque. French was the second language spoken in Beirut. I hadn't known this and was most impressed.

Our layover hotel was the five-star Phoenicia InterContinental, located directly across from the sea and the glitzy and famous Hotel St. Georges. (Okay, pencils at the ready for those of you still taking notes: The St. Georges was once *the* place to be, or be seen, for the glamour and glitz of the rich and famous: Richard Burton and Elizabeth Taylor were frequent guests and maintained a suite there. The Shah of Iran visited often. J. Paul Getty hung out at the pool. The St. Georges was also a magnet for rich Arab men who could come to Beirut and get away with all the things they couldn't get away with back in Baghdad, Riyadh or Kuwait City. One of those filthy-rich Arab men was a young Osama bin Laden who came to partake of all that was bacchanal and not taboo: free-flowing alcohol, drugs, rock music, rock-hard female flesh.

Even British spy turned Russian double agent, Kim Philby used the St. Georges as an office and watering hole to binge drink when he wanted to get out of his nearby flat on the Rue Kantari that he shared with Eleanor Brewer, ex-wife of former *New York Times* Middle East correspondent, Sam Brewer.)

When we checked into the Phoenicia, the hotel reception had me sharing a room with one of the stewardesses, until they realized their mistake and that "J. Breakfield" was a male. Everyone had a good laugh, but not me, I was crying my eyes out. The hotel was not used to seeing male flight attendants with Pan Am.

Before I went to find my room I had a little snoop about the hotel. Well, this was a far cry from our motel during Training! The Phoenicia was a twelve story structure of outstanding opulence. I had never stayed in a hotel of such grandeur before. I came upon a massive marble staircase that soared up for two stories. Coming down the staircase was a wave of serious looking businessmen in suits. A few others were dressed in military uniforms. I took a step back and let them sweep past. After they disappeared, I asked a bell boy what was going on.

"That's Juan Carlos, the future King of Spain."

* * *

I stepped out onto my balcony at the Phoenicia and took in a breath of sweet sea air. Everything was so romantic. And the view was like nothing I had ever seen before. In front of me was the gilded Corniche seafront. In the distance, pastel pinks and magentas danced on the horizon as the sun slipped into the shimmering Mediterranean. To the right, and off in the distance, mountains covered with snow rose majestically toward the heavens. On the bare bosoms of those mountains were the Cedars of Lebanon.

"Beirut!" I probably shouted it out loud. The playground of the glitterati and often called the Paris of the Middle East, for it was the singular city in the region offering everything Paris did: global financial institutions, state-of-the-art medical centers, grand museums, world-class universities, leading-edge aircraft maintenance facilities, jaunty sidewalk cafés, Michelin-rated restaurants—plus prostitutes and brothels galore.

I couldn't quite believe that I was actually here. One week I was pub crawling down NW 36th Street in Miami, and the next week I was exploring cosmopolitan and chic Beirut.

I glanced at the hotel next to ours. It was the Holiday Inn. Later that year, the bullet-riddled, shelled edifice of that hotel would appear daily on newscasts around the world as a symbol of gutted American interests in a war-torn country. A war was about to break out, but none of us had a clue there would be war. And none of us were aware of feuding factions. All we saw were palm trees, gin-clear waters and some of the most beautiful beaches in the world. If Beirut was the Paris of the Middle East, this coast was the French Riviera of the Middle East.

I cast my mind back to our arrival a few hours earlier. Why had there been armoured military carriers on the tarmac at the airport and soldiers carrying machine guns walking around the terminal?

My phone rang and I hurried back in to answer it.

"Meet us downstairs in forty-five minutes," came a voice with a lilting accent .

"Corolla?"

"The entire crew is going out to dinner. We've booked a table at a restaurant on Rue Hamra. You will be treated like a king. We will be your harem…"

I laughed.

"Why are you laughing?" Corolla teased.

* * *

One hour later, I was sitting on a Persian rug on the floor of a traditional Lebanese bistro.

All 21 of us, cockpit and cabin, had commandeered a section of the eatery, and we were sitting with our legs in the lotus position, occupying two low, long wooden tables.

Watching us from darkened recesses of the restaurant, were small groups of men smoking shisha.

I sat next to Corolla as she had clearly adopted me and had taken me under her wing. We drank a Château Ksara rosé wine from the southern Beqaa Valley, and we dined on an array of small dishes called *mezze*, which were essentially the Lebanese equivalent of tapas. These were various dishes with conflicting flavours, dishes that I had never heard of, such as: *hummus*, *tabbouleh*, *baba ghanouj*, grilled marinated seafood, skewered lamb and...goat. (Have you ever seen what goats eat? Puts you right off.)

Instead of using forks, we scooped up the delights with Lebanese flat bread.

For dessert, baklava with Attar syrup, halva, and coffee were offered, but Corolla and I stayed with the rosé. Some of the others passed on the dessert, but turned their attention to Arak, which is a moderately evil, somewhat frisky national drink in Lebanon that is anise-flavoured. It's served in ice-chilled cups, and resembles something you would donate at a sperm bank.

I remember being exceedingly happy, and I don't think it was just from the wine. And I just couldn't imagine wanting to do anything else with my life back then. Imagine, off in some exotic local, with like-minded folk, sharing adventure, basking in camaraderie, telling stories, laughing, glowing—a once in a lifetime opportunity.

It wasn't like this on every layover in the future, but more often than not, there were elements of it. Sure there were times when for assorted reasons members of the crew chose to keep to themselves, but often many of us did things together. We were a team, and as I've mentioned, a family. Perhaps that's why over forty years later, I'm still in contact with many of my old crew colleagues.

22

Caught Between a Hard Rock and Home

Seven days later, I was back in London.

I had survived my first trip. I felt inordinately more confident. And I was looking forward to my next adventure.

But I still had no place to live.

I stopped by Crew Briefing to check my mail box. No mail. I paid a visit to Graham in Scheduling. He had my schedule for the next month waiting for me. And I couldn't believe it: Another Delhi trip, six days off. New York, three days off. Amsterdam, two days off, and another Delhi.

If I remember correctly, we needed to fly a minimum of 67 hours. Soon, I would be packing over 80 hours into a month, and that could translate into lots of overtime and welcomed per diam.

"We've found a flat!"

I turned around. Standing there was Wendy Shepherd, from Australia.

"G'day, Jon, we need one more roommate. You in?"

Wendy, Rob Halkides, Anna-Lise Schwartz (Norway) and Vigdis Gjesdal (Norway and Class Three) had found a three bedroom flat halfway between the Earl's Court tube station and the Gloucester Road tube station. Vigdis rightly reserved the single room, as she was *senior* to the rest of us, by *one* whole week. Wendy and Anna-Lise would share a room, and Rob and I could share a room.

I was in.

The flat was furnished in minimalistic, rental-flat décor and was three steep flights up. After flying through the night, I often felt as if I were climbing the Hillary Step to get up to our sanctuary.

Our living room had an expansive bay window which looked out on to Collingham Gardens, an idyllic oasis that we never had the privilege of visiting as it was part of the "Key and lock gardens" of London. The famous 19th-century art critic, John Ruskin, said: "The measure of a city's greatness is to be found in the quality of its public spaces, its parks and squares." Regrettably, it seemed the access to London's greatness was the privilege of only a fortunate moneyed few.

I did some digging around (not in the garden, rather at the library) and unearthed the fact that the Borough of "Kensington and Chelsea," unsurprisingly, is the borough with the most private gardens in all of London, with more than 100 which are restricted to *residents' (owners) use only*.

* * *

To make our way to our flat from London Heathrow airport, we could take a bus to Hounslow West and catch the tube to Earl's Court. The tube didn't run all the way out to the airport from central London as it does now, and it could take anywhere from one hour to nearly two to get home. I could have chosen to live closer to the airport, but I was enraptured with London and it was imminently appealing to be living within walking distance of Hyde Park, Harrods, Covent Garden or Leicester Square, Soho and the West End.

Alternatively, we could catch the big red double-decker route-master BEA bus from just outside Terminal 2, which meant an icy, circuitous, freeze-your-face-off numbing walk from Terminal 3 for the right to queue in the unforgiving wind tunnel that was the bus pickup area. I could then ride all the way to the West London Air Terminal on Cromwell Road. This was often my first choice as I could nod off and let drool run down onto my uniform tie and not have to worry about changing trains or missing my stop. If we had to head to the airport in the wee hours of the morning, say 4am, we would book a mini-cab the night before, and these loyal drivers would often ring our doorbell to make sure we were awake. They had to work in the middle of the night and we had to work in the middle of the night and this formed a bond of respect and commiseration.

* * *

Looking back at our living situation, perhaps we were a bit spoiled for space. Five flight attendants in a three-bedroom flat seemed the right way to go at the time, but now I've heard of up to twenty F/As juggling sleeping arrangements in a flat the size of ours or smaller. And why not? Only twice during the first year in London were we all home at the same time. I never got to see my flatmates unless I was walking off the aircraft in Beirut, New Delhi, Bangkok or New York and they were walking on.

And that happened more often than you could imagine.

* * *

As I mentioned, the London base was quite small.

And one day I heard that they were in the hunt for pursers.

The idea of being a purser appealed to me. Better pay, a chance to build on my CV, and remember I was all about organization. I qualified easily enough, but my first trip was on a 707 and I had never flown or worked a 707 since Training.

Then things went pear-shaped.

When I turned up for the briefing, I learned that the senior purser had called in sick and I was suddenly not only going to be the only purser on the flight, I was *senior* purser, which meant I had to do the briefing to a crew of eight, all years more senior and experienced than I. We were flying off to Philadelphia with a full load and I thought I would *scheiße meine Hosen*.

Thank goodness "my crew" saw the desperation in my voice as I croaked out the particulars of the flight during the briefing. Somehow we made it to Philadelphia without the wings falling off, or the ovens exploding, and I was so grateful I took the entire crew to the movies and plied them with soft drinks and buckets of popcorn. The movie was *THE STING*, and we all agreed that Paul Newman was even more handsome in person, sleeping in First Class, than up on the big silver screen.

After six enlightening months of being London's most junior purser, I downgraded back to F/A as I wasn't able to hold a decent line as a purser, and as much as I enjoyed flying to Philadelphia, I was missing Beirut.

The next month I actually won the schedule I bid for and my first trip was back to Beirut, and on to Tehran and Delhi. When I turned up early for the briefing, I was pleased to find out that the In-flight Director was, yes, you've guessed, Muffy Harmar. In the months to come, it seemed every time I had a seven-day Delhi trip, Muffy would be the IFD.

I often cast my mind back to this particular trip for it became memorable on account of what happened in Tehran. We had landed safely and deplaned nearly a full-load of passengers. Muffy and I were standing by the open exit at L2. There was no jet-bridge, just the moveable stairs leading down. We were awaiting the arrival of new passengers and were admiring the snow on the mountains above Tehran, when we watched a Lufthansa 747 land, taxi along the taxiway and pull in next to us. Only he didn't just pull in next to us, he crashed into us. Not head-on, or T-bone, but a good bashing with his wing on ours. And Muffy and I had to hang on to keep from being thrown out the open exit door by our rocking-and-rolling aircraft.

Lufthansa suffered substantial damage to their wing and was going nowhere any time soon. Pan Am got off lucky and we were able to continue on to Delhi after only a short delay.

"Safer in the air, than on the ground," Muffy had so rightly noted.

* * *

If I won the monthly schedule I coveted, I often had a block of seven or eight days off in a row. I was so eager to see the world, I would ask Graham in Scheduling if I could pick up a trip and he always seemed to find me a three-day New York or Munich or Hamburg trip. If I had just two or three days off, I would walk London, albeit in a seriously jet-lagged stupor. It really is a grand city. I loved going to Harrods and hanging about in the Food Halls. I had never seen anything quite like this. One day I saw Katherine Hepburn with a bodyguard. On another occasion, I saw record and film producer John Rubin.

On one of the upper floors of Harrods, they sold pianos: uprights, baby grands and grands. I noticed a young man here, tuning the pianos, He worked with impressive focus and seemed, no pun intended, to be able to tune out the outer world and concentrate on his duty at hand.

The young piano tuner was blind.

* * *

Chelsea in 1973 was not what it is today. Same with Sloane Street and Sloane Square. There were no "Sloane Rangers," and it wasn't the poseurs' playground that it is now, it was just a quaint area where great deals could be found on both men's and women's clothing.

* * *

A new restaurant has opened in London recently. It set up shop in an old Rolls Royce car dealership, and it's the first of its kind anywhere in the world.

Are you ready for this?

It's called the Hard Rock Café.

And I'm going to see what all the word-of-mouth hullabaloo is about, but before I do so, let me just check the little notepad attached to our fridge. Hmmm: Rob was in Moscow and wouldn't be back for nearly a week. Wendy and Anna-Lise were on a ten-day trip to Bangkok and Vigdis was down in Africa.

I would be going to the Hard Rock alone. As flight attendants, we often did loads of things alone. Somewhat thrilling. Somewhat sad. We went to the movies alone, the theatre alone, to dinner alone. Worryingly, we even drank alone. *In a pub*, I'm talking, not at home like some sad sack. Sure, once you were married or in a relationship with someone who held down a normal job, you had a partner in crime to do all these fun things with, but not when you had no one in your life or your soul mate was a flight attendant, as well.

Unless you team bid.

I took the tube to Hyde Park Corner and cut over to green and leafy Hyde Park and ambled the circuitous way to the Hard Rock, and came down Old Park Lane past the Playboy Club. Long sentence, long walk around the block, but it was a warm and pleasant evening and well worth the extra effort. And then my eyes grew stalks: there was a queue to get in. Wow, opened a short time and already so popular. Who knew? Back in 1973, there was no indication that a quirky hamburger joint would mushroom into hundreds of even quirkier establishments around the globe in the form of restaurants, hotels, casinos and live music venues—with great T-shirts and sweatshirts.

Eventually I was able to penetrate the café and was guided to a seat by one of the two original ex-pat American owners. The gentleman stuck me in one of the booths over by tall windows which looked out onto Piccadilly.

I ordered a hamburger with fries. The price was not bad, certainly affordable, even for me. (At the time, the exchange rate was so awful, we were only getting one pound sterling by forking out $2.70. Honolulu had a base allowance, but we poor souls at the London base were not afforded such luxury, even though we were paid in dollars.) The burger arrived. It was massive. It didn't taste like any burger I had ever eaten in my life. Was that good or bad? Was that cause for concern? Have you ever done that? Ordered a country's distinctive cuisine, but in foreign land? I ordered schnitzel in New Delhi once, which you will soon hear about.

When I finished my burger and stepped outside, it was dark and London was alive with bright lights, and nattily dressed folk promenading and only a few panhandlers. I decided to walk a bit myself, and I did so all the way into the West End and the theatre district.

Gypsy was playing at the Piccadilly. I looked at my watch. It was almost time for Intermission.

I waited.

I lurked.

And I slipped in with all the legitimate patrons who had been hunkered down just out front having a fag.

* * *

After the curtain fell and the play was finished, and I hadn't been removed from the theatre and arrested, I leisurely strolled over to Leicester Square in a right balmy evening for London. That's when I hit the proverbial wall. Jet-lag was kicking in BIG TIME. I decided to splash out and take a taxi back to our flat.

I found one of those red iconic telephone boxes on the far corner of Leicester Square over by the Swiss House. The phone box was emblazoned with a royal crown above the door. Stuck to the glass inside were five business cards for Escort Services. And two for local cab companies: West End Taxis, and Hackney Hackneys.

I'd never made a phone call from a public phone booth in England and I wasn't sure about the procedure. I read the instructions. More confused than ever now. Apparently, I had to balance a tuppence in the little coin slot, dial the number, and wait for the "PIPS."

What were PIPS?

Weren't they found in fruit?

I balanced a two-pence coin in the little slot, then came a shrill and ear-bleeding BEEP! BEEP! BEEP!

I heard a voice on the other end bleat "Hello, Hackney Hackneys?"

And I panicked.

"Hackney Hackneys?" the voice repeated.

"Wait! Don't go!" I started to talk then remembered the coin. Was I meant to push it in? I pushed. The coin didn't go in.

"Hackney Hackneys?"

If I could hear the man perhaps I didn't need to force the bloody coin in. "I would like to book a…

And the line went dead.

I tried again, and again, but I was now so wired, I decided to walk home.

PIPS. WHAT THE HELL ARE PIPS?

23

New Uniforms, *sadly*

As Pan Am flight attendants, we were always known for being impeccably coiffed and smartly attired.

And now we were getting a uniform change.

Academy Award winner Edith Head (*eight* Oscars!) has designed our new uniform and I have to say right up front that I preferred the old one. The uniform, not Edith Head, although her hair could've done with a makeover.

Our original "pilot" shirts had fit better and looked as if we actually worked for an airline. The new shirts were curiously cut and looked as if we worked in a call centre. If I spilled the coq-au-vin on my old uniform, it would clean up quite nicely with a little splash of fizzy soda water. If I did that on my new uniform, it looked as if I had spilled a Sunday carvery on it and had chosen to ignore it. The trousers on the old uniform fit better, as well. That and we had a cool belt. With the new uniform, I felt as if I worked 9-5 in an office—something I was trying to avoid doing—by working for an airline.

Might I just point out here that the new uniforms for the female flight attendants were extremely attractive and the envy of the industry. The females had two different uniforms: one a galaxy gold, the other in Pan Am blue.

Edith Head famously uttered these words regarding the female flight attendants' attire, hinting at the breadth of sexuality: "Your dresses should be tight enough to show you're a woman and loose enough to show you're a lady."

24

Once There Were Only Stewards

Juan Trippe had the vision to operate flying boats so his pilots could land in the harbours, rivers, and lagoons of cities that did not have an airport, the same way he had landed in the still waters behind the sand dunes on Coney Island and Fire Island with his war surplus "floatplanes."

That solved a myriad of logistical problems and the need to cut runways out of impenetrable jungle or coral.

And this is one of the reasons there were only male flight attendants at the time. The job of the steward, are you ready, was to row passengers out to the seaplane and steady the boat as the punters clambered onboard. Off in exotic and distant, mosquito-infested locales, the stewards had to sweat and strain to schlepp and load baggage. They even had to shop for the gourmet delicacies they would need for the next leg of their trip. Try that sometime, go off to the back of beyond and find all the items you will need for your fancy-smancy dinner party that evening.

* * *

As prohibition lingered, giving everyone a good case of the shakes, moneyed Americans were desperate to escape their twitchy-limbed, law-abiding neighbours, so they flew Pan Am to Havana for booze, a good time, and to misbehave.

Passengers might have sincerely desired to go to Havana to have a mojito, daiquiri or Singapore Sling, but they were not so very keen on flying 90 miles over open water. Consequently, Pan Am had difficulty booking ALL EIGHT SEATS on each flight. Can you imagine? I can just hear it: "What's it look like today?"

"We've got a full load. We've got *eight*."

Besides passengers' trepidation of flying over water, they were not so very impressed when they finally made it to Havana and, say the El Floridita Bar, and witnessed the drunken behavior and bravado of the unshaven, rheumy-eyed pilots in well-worn leather aviator jackets On occasion, the pilots would even boldly dare passengers who had come over on the boat to fly back with Pan Am.

Back in Miami, Pan Am's selling point was much more subtle: **"FLY WITH US TO HAVANA, AND YOU CAN BATHE IN BARCARDI RUM TWO HOURS FROM NOW."**

Propelled by the swashbuckling behavior of his pilots, Juan Terry Trippe coined the phrase: "You must demand excellence," and dictated that everything about Pan Am must be the best. When other pilots and air crew were still allowed to fly in tatty leather jackets or suspect civilian dress, he demanded that his crews wore spotless naval style uniforms, white uniform caps, and he called his new planes "Clippers," so named after the glamorous sailing ships of the 19th century.

Crew were not allowed to smoke or drink in public nor even appear in public without their jackets and ties.

Pan Am flight-line services set the standard for the rest of industry.

In the pursuit of excellence, Pan Am became a cultural icon of the 20th century. In an era dominated by flag carriers that were wholly or majority government-owned, Pan Am was also the unofficial flag carrier of the United States.

In its first year, Pan Am flew passengers between Florida and Cuba, extended its routes southward to Haiti and San Juan, and eventually expanded until it reached deeper into the Caribbean, Central and South America.

Pan Am was in the air, but so was change, by 1960, stewards were nearly a thing of the past and cabin crews were almost exclusively female.

Stay tuned, this feature would have far-reaching consequences for me when I arrived on the scene in 1973.

25

And You, Sir, POOOFFF! You Are a Wee Piece of Shite!

Flash forward from Juan Trippe's statement "YOU MUST DEMAND EXCELLENCE" and come with me on Pan Am's Round-the-World Flight Two, eastbound.

We were on final approach into the sphincter-puckering nightmare that was Hong Kong's Kai Tak International Airport and the checkerboard had just come into sight (just after spying the laundry blowing from the rooftop apartments down below us). Stan Oliver and I were seated on the jump seat just across from "Zelda" (perhaps not her real name).

Zelda was a hard-core Glaswegian, yet could easily switch into a posh strain of Glaswegian—if there was such a thing—and she had worked for the airline for so long, she knew what she could get away with and what she couldn't, no scarf and an extra button or two undone. Perhaps a cheeky hemline.

One of the other areas where Zelda pushed the envelope with the Pan Am logo on it was with her hair and make-up. Zelda's hair was dyed platinum and was so out-of-this-universe wild, she could get FM radio reception. Her eyes were blushed lavishly in a raccoon-esque smash of violet, her eyelashes could have doubled as floor sweepers and her lips were fashionably encircled with some unknown tint that may have been the latest big thing at Harrod's or Selfridges or Macys, but was in distinct conflict with Pan Am's standard Revlon Persian Melon.

How did she get away with it? Why wasn't she reprimanded? Didn't she worry about getting sacked? Having said that, I don't remember Zelda looking like that during the briefing back in Bangkok. Perhaps she went just a bit rogue downline when the exit doors were closed and cross-checked? Some flight attendants did that, you know, went rogue when they were light years from home base. At least Zelda still used the jet bridges and moveable stairs, and hadn't deployed the escape slide to deplane.

Not yet, anyway.

Zelda was sitting on her jump seat, making the announcements in flawless Japanese. Yes, *Japanese*. Somewhere in the middle of the announcements, Stan nudged me and motioned with his head towards a Clipper Class passenger who was the *spitting* image of a young Muammar Gaddafi, indeed, sort of the male equivalent of coyote ugly. He was staring at Zelda's spread legs, looking up her dress (trying to get a shot at her Victoria's Secrets). You see, Zelda always squirmed when she made the announcements and when she squirmed her legs involuntarily flapped open and shut.

Emphasis on the open.

Mo Coyote-Gaddafi had spent most of the journey making passes, spewing innuendoes and snapping his fingers impatiently "Whiskey! Whiskey!" at the younger stewardesses onboard, Janie Hulton, in particular. But Janie didn't suffer fools, and she had quickly lost her patience with him. When Mo Co snapped his fingers at Janie one time too many and pointed imploringly at the little round air vent just above his head, easily within reach, Janie had had enough. She marched up to the arrogant sod and said: "See this little vent? You can do this all on your own. You just reach that snapping little hand of yours, put it on this vent, and YOU JUST SCREW IT!"

That was Janie's run-in, but now, *shudder*, Mo Co was about to tread on a Glaswegian, and no one fucks with a Weegie lassie.

No one.

Zelda had just finished her announcements when she saw this slavering excuse for the male of the species lean farther out in the aisle to get an unobstructed, frequent-flyer view.

"Oi, laddie!" Zelda screamed in guttural Glaswegian over the intercom, spreading her legs wide open. "Ye wanna look up here, ye jobby bawbag? Take a good hard look!"

First of all, Stan and I couldn't believe our ears, second of all, we couldn't believe our eyes, because we had never seen someone from the Middle East turn the colour green before.

The entire cabin froze and there was not a sound to be heard from the moment the plane's tires screeched on touchdown until we had pulled up to the gate. During this time we noticed that Mo Co was now metamorphosing from a rich green into a burning shade of red.

"Thank you very much for flying with us today," chirped Zelda, her vernacular magically transformed as the passengers from First Class disembarked. "See you again. Bye. Ba-bye. Taraa…"

"A real pro," Stan noted.

Many in Clipper Class didn't budge, remaining undoubtedly attentive, waiting to see what Mo Co was going to do.

Finally, he decided to bolt. When he saw his only way out was blocked by Zelda, he must have decided to go on the attack because he charged right at her.

"Look at that hair of yours!" he cried, rudely sticking a finger in Zelda's face. "Look at your eye make-up! Look at that lipstick! Why, you look like a…a…a witch! Yes, that's what you are. You are nothing more than a WITCH!!!"

Zelda just stared calmly back.

Stunned silence all around.

Then Zelda spoke and when she spoke, this remarkable lady spoke pearls, Second-City-of-the-Empire pearls: "You know, Training School was a long time ago for me, but I'll never forget what we learned. In Training School, we were taught that the passenger is always right, oh, aye. And you know what? You are right, I am a witch. And you, sir, POOOFFF! You are a wee piece of shite!"

The passengers gasped. Mo Co appeared to have been struck mute by lightning and it was all he could do to remove his charred remains from the aircraft.

Stan and I watched him go. We looked at Zelda who was now studying her fuchsia nails. She glanced over at us, then at the remaining passengers and gave them a big, victorious smile.

And with that, everyone burst into spontaneous applause.

26

An Unwelcomed Visitor

Summer is upon us again, and I must say London is an exceedingly handsome city this time of the year with flowers and trees in full bloom, and the heady fragrance of the many floral wonders. Having said that, it was 90 degrees Fahrenheit when we departed New York last night, and it was 58 degrees when we landed in London this morning.

Summer, indeed.

It felt as if I were climbing Everest again (without oxygen this time) as I dragged my bag up the three flights of stairs to our flat. I looked at my watch: 7.45am. *Ugh.* These long trips through the night and through time zone after time zone were taxing and always took their toll. But the thought of a deep, warm bed waiting for me always seemed to save the day. And I never felt guilty diving into my bed and snoozing all day. None of us did.

I just made it to our flat only to find the rarest of instances when all of my roommates were home. Which I was thrilled with. What I wasn't thrilled with, they were all standing there glaring at me.

"Good day to you, too!" I said to all the glowering faces.

"Sarah is here!" hissed Vigdis.

I wracked my brain. "Who's Sarah?"

"And her roommate!" hissed Rob.

"Who are these people? And stop hissing at me."

"You know damn well, Jon," Wendy hissed. "You shouldn't have invited friends of yours without consulting us first. They've been here for two days already."

"But I don't know anyone named Sarah."

"She said she's from L.A., where you went to university," Anne-Lisa hissed.

"Oh, no, not that Sarah!"

"An old girlfriend?"

"No, my bank teller. The only deposit I ever made with her was an unemployment check. I didn't invite her."

"Well, she's here!" they all hissed.

"I'll go have a talk with her. Where is she?"

"In your bed."

"My bed!" I hissed. "Wait till I get my hands on her."

"I think that's exactly what she has in mind, Jon," Rob smirked.

I walked down the long hall which led to the bedroom I shared with Rob and opened the door. Sarah was curled up in my bed. In Rob's bed was a big lump letting out little porcine-like snores.

I closed the door and walked back down the hall where Rob had taken up refuge. "They're unconscious in there and the roommate is sawing serious wood in your bed!"

Rob raised four fingers, roommate sign language for *Tell Me About It.* "I slept on the couch last night. Why don't we just go strangle the two of—" Rob was interrupted.

"Hi, Jon…"

I turned around and standing down at the end of the hall, in her black-and-white spotted pajamas, was my bank teller. Standing behind her, looking decidedly jet-lagged, was her traveling companion.

"What a nice surprise," I said, my teeth superglued together.

Sarah yawned. "This is my roommate, Frenchy. That's her real name." Frenchy yawned, gave us a good shot at her velum, then turned and waddled into the kitchen. "Awfully sorry about just turning up like this," Sarah lumbered on. "It's just that we arrived in London and didn't know where to go." Long beat. Awkward silence. "It's really nice to see you, though, I must admit." Big smile. Lots of flapping eyelashes. Frightening subtext.

"How'd you get this address?"

"You gave it to me at the bank."

"I did?"

"You said you were working with Pan Am in London."

"I did?"

"Yes, you were very proud. You said if I ever was in London to stop by."

"I did?"

"And you gave me your address."

"I did?" I said, hearing the refrigerator door open. "So how's the bank?"

"Who can think about the bank when I'm here—in Europe!"

I glanced at my roommates.

"Do you mind if we take a shower?" Sarah said. "We would love to stay, but we really should leave for France today. Frenchy's never been."

"Let me get you some towels," I said, greatly relieved.

"No need, we borrowed some of yours already."

Long beat. Deafening silence. "Listen, Sarah, I'm going to go to breakfast with my roommates. We'll see you in a little while."

"Okay, I'd better say goodbye now. We could be gone when you come back."

"Well, at least we were able to enjoy your company for a little while," I said, wondering why in the hell I said that.

As we moved down the hall toward the front door, Rob offered this scary observation: "Says she's leaving, but it seems to me she'd rather stay and jump your bones."

Clearly, Sarah was taking advantage of a situation and my roommates had taken a little excursion into inconsiderate tourist hell. I wanted to go collapse, but I felt bad for my flatmates. I decided to try to restore their faith in me by blatantly bribing them with caffeine and grease.

There was the quaint Olde Worlde Café just off Old Brompton Road. I had been attracted to the little beanery because of the colourful clientele who frequented it, the warm people who ran it and an interesting sign near the loo which generously queried: "Need a nappy for your nipper?"

Plus the fayre was beyond scrumptious: a full English breakfast was served complete with fried eggs, fried potatoes, fried black pudding, fried tomatoes, toast, fried bread, jams and jellies, and steaming pots of coffee and tea—and of course there were the fried bacon rashers and the bangers. Everyone loved the rashers and bangers, even Rob who fell asleep at the table. This was nothing new, falling asleep at the table. Or in a bar. We were always in a somnolent state, and it didn't seem to matter where you were or what you were doing. Rob told me that only the week before, he had fallen asleep during Fellatio (*Fellatio* was the name of a one-act play at a nearby experimental theatre).

By the time we returned home from the fry-up, I was in a numbed daze from jet lag and cholesterol-overload. I remember going into the bathroom, undoing my tie, taking off my uniform shirt and it was just when I was dropping my drawers and looking forward to getting my dogs in a nice hot bath—that I heard the giggling.

Lounging in my bathtub, staring up at me, was Sarah.

I bolted.

When Sarah eventually exhumed herself from her bubble bath, she came into the front lounge and announced: "Frenchy and I had a fight. She went off on the hovercraft to France. I'm going to Amsterdam—tomorrow."

Wendy and Anna-Lise were flying off to Karachi later that day, and Rob and I ended up having to use their room that night since Sarah was still squatting in ours and neither of us wanted to end up in there with her behind closed doors.

I awoke the next morning disoriented, dopey and still jet-lagged. But for once I was prepared. I had a remedy. A nice Tetley's tea steeped for an eternity. Then I wouldn't feel disoriented any longer, just dopey and jet-lagged.

I was in the kitchen, rummaging through the cupboard wondering where my last bag of Tetley's had gone, when Sarah walked in sipping a cup of tea. "I could get used to this," she purred.

"Used to what?"

"Oh, just used to all this. *Europe.*"

For some unknown reason, when she said this, my mouth gave off that involuntary reflex your cat does when it spots a bird (and wants to kill it).

When I recovered, I excused myself with the pretext I was going for a walk.

As I walked down the three flights to the street level, I thought about 1665 when the Great Plague ravaged London, the next year the Great Fire destroyed London, during World War II, London suffered heavily from German incendiary bombs and parachute mines.

Now it was Sarah.

To rid the cobwebs and escape from my own home, I decided I needed a long walk. Long walks are agreeable in London as London is simply so vast. Because of clay soil (lousy for building tall buildings which scrape the sky) and because of good transportation, London has expanded horizontally. Now, if you feel like taking a little stroll, you have a city which covers half the size of the state of Rhode Island. What makes London particularly attractive is that even with all this "city" surrounding you, the Londoner is seldom far from grass and flowers. There are those great many glorious parks and hundreds of adorably small squares.

The temperature had already rocketed up into the low seventies and my stroll today took me down past the Royal Albert Hall where I entered Hyde Park near Knightsbridge. Hyde Park can be quite fetching, for despite its heavy patronage, it manages to maintain an air of rural tranquility. I crossed the leafy expanse along the Serpentine and headed over to Portobello Road. I enjoyed the buskers and craftspeople and musicians. I bought some flowers from some character known as "The Flower Man," listened to some Rasta guy playing a steel drum, tossed 50p in a homeless person's upturned bowler, "Ta Guv'nor and God bless," and then returned to my flat.

Back home I wanted to use the telephone to book a minicab for my next flight, but Sarah was on the phone. And she was on for as long as it takes to read the Bible, in Braille. After she rang off, she just shrugged her shoulders and smiled, "California. My parents."

"That was nice of them to call."

"I called them."

"Collect?"

"No, I don't want to take advantage of them. Don't worry about the call though. I'll be sure to leave some money before I go."

I'll believe that when I see it, is what I was thinking, but "When are you heading out?" is what I said.

"Looks like early tomorrow morning now. Are the flowers for me?"

I was flying off to New York on a three-day pattern, and I was glad to be seeing the last of Sarah. Besides, I hoped to catch a Broadway play in New York. If the flight was on schedule, I would have just enough time to check into the Berkshire and then hurry down to the theatre district where I could usually bribe an usher with a tenner. (My goal was one play per pay check.) If the plane was delayed or my funds were low, I would employ stealth by way of my newly learned "second acting" technique.

We had a smooth crossing of the pond and my layover in New York was a good one, I discovered a new bookstore on Lexington Avenue, Dr. Brown's Cream Soda and saw *A Little Night Music*. When Glynis Johns sang "Send In The Clowns," I thought of Sarah and Frenchy.

On my flight back to London, I met a new flight attendant on the trip. Her name was Pernilla and she had golden-blond hair and more freckles than a St. Tropez beach has topless bathers. Pernilla commuted to our London base from Copenhagen. This I was sad to learn. What I wasn't sad to learn was by the time we arrived back in London, Penilla had missed her connection to Copenhagen. So I invited her to stay at our place. "We always have a free bed at our flat."

Pernilla accepted.

When Pernilla and I arrived at the flat, we were barely in

the door when Vigdis came hurrying up to us.

"Vigdis, this is Pernilla," I said. "She missed her flight back to Copenhagen. I've offered her one of our free beds for the night."

Vigdis smiled and greeted Pernilla in English (nobody from Norway understands Danish) and then uttered these horrifying words, "She's still here! The bitch is still here."

"Sarah!"

"Yes, Sarah."

"Who's Sarah?" Pernilla wanted to know.

"My bank teller," I said.

I turned to Vigdis. "But, she was supposed to leave a couple days ago. What's her story this time?" Before Vigdis could speak, I heard a voice that was becoming like the "daaa duh... daaa duh..." in *JAWS*, signaling the shark's arrival.

"Hi, Jon..."

I turned to see Sarah standing in the doorway of my bedroom clothed only in a dress shirt—one of my Pan Am dress shirts!

"Sorry about still being here, but I'm waiting for my parents to wire me some money. Who's that?"

"This is Pernilla."

"Oh," was all she said, then she swam back into my bedroom.

I turned to Pernilla. "I guess you'll have to sleep in Wendy and Anna-Lise's room."

"No go, Jon," Vigdis informed me. "They're coming in from Istanbul today."

"The couch?"

"Rob's on the couch," Vigdis said forlornly.

"My room," came a distant voice. "She can share with me tonight," Sarah bleated.

27

Encore à **Beirut**

Beirut.

I couldn't believe I was back in Beirut.

To reach Lebanon, we had departed London in the wee hours, flew one hour to Frankfurt, spent about an hour on the ground picking up passengers (and oddly a cargo of frozen frogspawn), then flew two hours or so to Istanbul and spent another hour on the ground picking up more passengers. After all this, we still had two and a half more hours to Beirut. By the time we arrived in Beirut, it was late in the afternoon, local, and we had been given the unwelcomed news that some inexplicable green slime had leaked all over our crew bags.

As always, I had a room to myself.

Not that it was doing me any good, mind you.

I stepped out onto my balcony and watched a sailboat on the Mediterranean for a moment and then hurried back into my hotel room. Because I had just showered, I was wearing only a towel around my waist. Perhaps half-naked men running around the balconies weren't condoned in this part of the world.

I sat on my bed and stared at a little white light connected to my telephone. This light was my link to the outside world. This light dictated my life. When the little white light flashed it meant that I had a message, and a message usually meant Airline Operations wanted to tell me if there was a delay, or in this case, inform me where I would be flying to next. I had been "positioned" in Beirut. I was simply there awaiting assignment. It amazed me how Pan Am scheduling could keep track of all the crew members stuck in the four corners of the world before the days (and nights) of computers and Microsoft. The next day the rest of my crew would fly on to

Karachi and Delhi. But I didn't know if I would be flying eastbound or westbound. Longitudinal logistics were Ping-Ponging in my mind, when I heard the knock.

I tightened my towel and toddled to the door.

"Jon? Are you there?" came a familiar voice.

I opened the door. It was Karolina, one of the flight attendants I had flown in with today, and she was looking cute in her white short-shorts and skimpy halter top. Karolina was from Prague and was dark and lithe and had strikingly good looks. Czech, mate?

"Have you had dinner yet?" Karolina asked, her eyes lazily checking me out in my towel. "You're the only one I know in the crew."

"Let me just throw on some clothes," I said, marvelling at my good fortune.

"Okay, you dress. I'll wait."

But I was the one waiting. I was waiting for Karolina to leave so I could get dressed, but she wouldn't leave the room. Finally, she went to the window and looked off in the direction of the Hotel St. Georges.

We found a restaurant down near the wharf with a menu fifteen pages long and containing 365 entrées (really). It was a small restaurant and as was custom we sat yoga-style on a thick-piled Persian carpet with our legs curled under a table which was no more than a foot-and-a-half high. And there weren't any doors leading to or from the dining room, just oriental carpets hanging down from the door frames.

We ordered in French, and feasted on *fattouch* and *tabouli* and *shwarma* and *bastirma* and *hummus*, and drank glass after glass of provincial Château Musart rosé wine. It seemed every time our glasses were empty the proprietor of the restaurant would magically appear with his carafe and refill our glasses.

"They say this wine is grown near the Beqaa."

"Really? I thought that's where they grew terrorists."

"You make me laugh," Karolina said, then she threw back more of the rosé.

The wine made Karolina talkative. And when she talked

her lips parted, then pursed, and like some great sucking creature drew me nearer and nearer to her. "I was born in Prague. My father is member of the Prague Philharmonic. He still lives there."

"And your mother?"

"She lives in Tarrytown, New York. My parents are divorced. I came to America with my mother. My younger brother stayed with my father."

"Do you ever get to see your father and brother?"

"Often—that's why I work with the airline."

Karolina looked at me and peered deep into my soul.

Would I finally find romance in Beirut of all places?

After dinner we took a long walk through Beirut's gold market. At a shop called Joe's Interline we both made insignificant gold purchases. (Gold was around a hundred dollars an ounce and rings, bracelets and necklaces, in eighteen carat, were quite affordable. In Lebanon, all gold bore the symbol of the cedar tree and was rated .75, equal to eighteen carats or seventy-five percent of twenty-four carat.)

We left the bustling gold market behind and swayed down clogged Rue Hamra, past pounding nightclubs and darkened movie theatres. The night was on the balmy side of steamy and strolling through the streets of Beirut was like walking through a combination of paradise and a used Mercedes-Benz parking lot. Even the taxis were Mercedes. We stopped at a little sidewalk café. It was clearly a male bastion. The men were drinking strong glutinous coffee and smoking from coiled hukas. They watched our every move as we ate almond cookies and drank some of the glutinous coffee.

I looked over at Karolina. It was so romantic sitting here with her in a quirky café in a far-flung part of the world. I had always travelled alone, but now I was beginning to wonder if this is what it could be like travelling with a partner in crime.

"Do you prefer to travel alone or with someone?" I asked.

"I've always travelled by myself," Karolina said, "but I think that's about to change…"

My head snapped up. "How?"

"I think I'm going to start team-bidding with my boyfriend."

28

Left to Rot in Beirut

The next morning the little white light still wasn't flashing. What was going on? Why wasn't I being sent somewhere? I guess it didn't matter. My head hurt from provincial rosé. And my heart hurt because Karolina already had someone in her life.

I looked over at the little white light again. When the light started flashing, I would have an hour before I had to be downstairs in the lobby of the hotel to be picked up by the crew bus. This little window of freedom afforded me the opportunity to do short sorties out into the streets of Beirut—to explore.

And I paid quite a few visits to the swimming pool watching the Lebanese woman strut around the pool area in their bikinis and high heels. I had never seen this combination before, and it sure made their legs look great. I remember standing by the pool one morning as one of the bikini-clad beauties stilettoed by. An older Frenchman standing near me (who resembled Yves Montand) whistled and said to the young lady, *"Jolies jambes!"* Then he turned to me and said in an avuncular sort of way: "A man may say 'nice legs,' but the woman knows he's really looking at her derrière."

I made a mental note of this.

On my second day of waiting for my little white light, I went waterskiing out in front of the St. George Hotel. The Mediterranean always seemed to be glassy here and for seven Lebanese pounds, I could ski until it was time to hurry back to my room to check for messages. There were no messages, so I took more short walks through the palm-lined streets of Beirut. I don't remember feeling or seeing any tension between the multi-sectarian population, I just remember it being exotically attractive and oppressively hot.

On day three, I went waterskiing again, but still no white light, still no assignment. It was as if Pan Am had forgotten I was there. New crews arrived and departed on a daily basis. I saw them pass through the hotel, and I greeted them, and I chatted with them, but I never left with them.

Then one day the crews stopped coming.

And I'm not one to be an alarmist, but when you are off in Beirut, *positioned*, waiting for your next flight and suddenly there is no next flight, you start to get a wee bit tense.

What happened to Pan Am? What was happening in Beirut? Did somebody know something I didn't?

"Hi, this is Jon Breakfield..." As much as I enjoyed waterskiing, admiring the girls by the pool and drinking melt-your-face-off coffee, I figured it was time to ring up "Operations" in London.

"Hang on a moment, Breakfield," a tiny voice squawked back through the receiver.

I hung on.

Then I heard a voice scream into my ear, "Breakfield! It's Graham in Scheduling. Where the bloody hell are you?!"

"Beirut."

"Beirut!!! Crikey, we lost track of you. We've got to get you out of there."

He asked me to hang on again. I hung on again. Why did they have to get me out? What possibly could be so urgent?

Our fearless scheduler, Graham, who was usually as cool as the back side of your pillow, sprang back on the line. "Listen carefully, Jon. Get your arse out to the airport NOW! Flight 2 will be evacuating some of our station people. You've got to get on this airplane. There's an explosive situation in Beirut that's about to erupt any minute. This may be our last flight out. The aircraft will be on the ground in just over an hour. Got it? One hour."

"Last bloody flight out!" I yelled, as I hung up the phone. I grabbed my bag (which was always packed) and blew downstairs and outside. There was nobody at the pool, no one water skiing over at the St. Georges, and the town suddenly looked different. Everything seemed more subdued. Everything seemed like a Sunday morning. I hailed a taxi. "*Monsieur, à l'aéroport, s'il vous plaît.*"

"No go airport," the driver said, waving a finger sideways at me. "No go airport." And he sped off.

I hailed another taxi and he, too, refused to take me to the airport. I waited. And waited. Suddenly, in a town that had looked as if a taxicab convention was taking place—there were no more taxis.

A nerve-racking twenty minutes went by. No takers. Nothing. I went back into the hotel and asked the front desk to ring a cab for me. They did. I went back outside to wait. Almost immediately, a taxi came, but he wouldn't take me to the airport either. *Crikey!* Finally I stuck out my thumb at the next set of wheels that drove by. The car was a rust-bucket. Something out of *Mad Max*, but with tires that were more bald. In it were four Lebanese teenagers. The rust-bucket screeched to a stop.

"I gotta get to the airport. Now. I'll pay you to take me out there."

The driver saw that I was wearing a uniform. "You work Pan Am?"

"Yes, Pan Am."

The driver, who looked like he could be the leader of a Lebanese street gang, turned to his filed-tooth buddies and said something to them in inner-city Arabic. Then he turned back to me and shot me a funny grin with curious subtext.

"Okay, cowboy, you come."

I hopped in the back seat and saw—that there was no back seat—just a grotty mattress. So, suddenly, here I was, sitting on a stained mattress, in a car that even junkyards would refuse, with four fledgling thugs. What the hell had I done?

As we lurched away from the curb the driver turned up the radio and blared out on tinny speakers, some wailing, warbling Lebanese classic. "Was big hit this song. Big hit," the driver informed me. And on this, all four of them started singing along to their type of music—music different from anything I had ever heard on KISS-FM, in L.A.

"You like?" asked the driver, watching me closely in the rear-view mirror.

"I like," I answered (trying to envision the video), and the driver hung a right and cut down some litter-strewn, narrow side street, with tall, cement, ripe-for-demolition slums on both sides.

We entered a rotting, rundown section of Beirut which seemed to lead to nowhere. The streets were pocked with potholes and tissue-like detritus was blowing everywhere. How could this be the way to the airport? Where was I being taken? I had placed myself in the hands of a band of future terrorists who used a mattress for a back seat, and I was being hustled off to a part of town which seemed like a good place to dump a body. The area was a desperate cliché of poverty: A rank sewage canal ran down the middle of the street. Laundry hung grey and lifeless from most balconies. Scrawny dogs barked menacingly at us as only scrawny dogs in books or films do. We careened around a corner and then another, and without warning the driver slammed on the brakes and we skidded to a halt in front of a house which could have easily been featured in the glossy pages of *Good Terrorist Housekeeping*.

"You want see my house?"

I did not like the sound of this nor the impromptu stop.

"Sorry, don't have time. Gotta get to the airport."

"No take long. Come take look."

"No."

"Yes. You come. You look."

I thought about yelling for help, but now the street seemed to be mysteriously barren of life forms. Even the scrawny dogs were suddenly on hiatus. I could run, but if I ran, I would be hopelessly lost in the Beirut equivalent of, well, Beirut.

"Okay," I said, grabbing my bag and climbing out of the car. "Let's make it quick."

"Bag okay in car. You leave there," said the driver. "After

you," and I was ushered to go first.

Scared witless, I stepped inside, certain I would never see the light of the Hard Rock Café again.

It took my eyes a long moment to adjust to the darkness. While I was waiting for them to adjust, my sense of smell took over. The air was stuffy, dank and dead. I peered through a dusty fog of airborne spores and rogue motes and the four youths were just coming into focus—standing behind me, just staring. As my eyes adjusted further I saw an unkempt house with windows but no glass and only a few pieces of furniture. No beds, just more suspect mattresses dotting the corners of the large room. Were they squatting? There may have been a bathroom or a hotplate somewhere, but I didn't see anything which resembled such luxury. On the wall above one mattress was an old poster. The poster was of medical student Che Guevara and his best friend Alberto Granado, a biochemist, when they were young men. Che Guevara and his friend were on a raft that had been given to them by the lepers they treated down in the Peruvian rainforest in the Amazon basin. It's a powerful image.

"Is this where you sleep?" I asked the driver.

"Yes, I sleep," he answered.

"You know who that is?" I asked, pointing to the poster.

"Yes," said the driver. The driver looked around at the interior of his dingy home with pride and turned to me. "So, what you think of my house?"

"I like," I replied. "I like very much."

A smile as wide as the soon-to-be Green Line swept across his young face. "Okay, we go now. We get you to airport—fast!"

We hurried outside past some grubby children (who had magically materialized) playing soccer in the street, and I could never put into words what was racing through my mind at that moment. These young men of Beirut weren't future terrorists, and they weren't killers, at least not then. They were simply young men, like me, but from a different end of the earth, who wanted to share a little bit of what was theirs.

Back in the car, we quit the part of the town which seemed on life support and eventually emerged on the beach road.

As we roared along adjacent to the sea, I noticed every mile or so there was a tank with a soldier. The soldiers were sitting on the turrets, manning machine guns. I was particularly unnerved when we drove only a few feet from one of the Soviet-built tanks and the soldier trained the barrel of the machine gun on us as we passed.

"Why the tanks?" I asked, as the music was turned off. "Why the machine gun aimed at us?" But nobody answered me. We drove in silence the rest of the way, past the sprawling Palestinian refugee camps and out to the airport.

When we arrived at the airport I jumped out of the car and went around to the driver's side. I regarded the driver, and he looked back at me for the longest time, envious perhaps that I was going to be able to board an airplane and go somewhere—anywhere. I handed him the rest of the Lebanese pounds I had.

The driver looked down at the money, then back up at me. "You keep. You keep so you remember Beirut." A handsome smile flashed across his face. Then he said, "Okay, I keep." We both laughed, and on that he turned his blaring music back on and screeched away and back toward his run-down home in his down-market section of Beirut.

I watched my new friends go, then turned and faced an airport absolutely teeming. There were agitated people everywhere, even on the flat rooftop. I had to push through the throngs to get to the outdoor Immigration checkpoint. I had almost reached the gate when I heard a distant rumbling. I turned and saw, coming in low over the Mediterranean and flying parallel to the beach, one of the most sincerely joyous sights you could possibly imagine. It was Pan Am Flight 2. As the prodigious 747 touched down with a screech of its tires, I saw the American flag painted atop its high-rising tail. The plane had made it in—and I was going to make it out.

I waited anxiously near the checkpoint. Off by our aircraft

I saw two of our flight attendants descend the moveable stairs to the tarmac. And I recognized them both. The taller woman with the riotous red hair was the In-flight Director. I had flown with her before. Her name was Siobhan, and she was from Londonderry in Northern Ireland. The other flight attendant, with the killer legs, was Bella.

"Jon!" Siobhan shouted as they moved through Immigration and over to landside.

"Siobhan! Bella!" Was I ever happy to see them. "What the hell's going on around here?"

"Troubles are comin'. Derry on a Saturday night, this place'll be lookin' like," Siobhan said.

"We're flyin' on to Delhi," added Bella.

"Can't be any worse than here."

Come along, Jon," Siobhan said, hurrying me. "Let's get you through security."

Together, we went over to the crew checkpoint when suddenly out of nowhere someone swung a rifle at me like a baseball bat and hit me across my chest. The blow sent me reeling backwards, almost knocking me to the ground. Screams erupted from everywhere and as I struggled to my feet, fists at the ready, all I could see was the end of a rifle pointing directly in my face.

"*Ante! Ante! Achreg men alchesh!*" shouted a Lebanese soldier. "You! You! Out of line! Now!"

"But he's with us!" screamed Siobhan.

"He's crew, ye daft bugger!" Bella added.

People crowded around pushing and shoving. The atmosphere was charged and dangerous.

"YOU OUT OF LINE!" repeated the soldier not wanting to back down and still pointing the rifle in my face. Other soldiers keyed on the commotion and hurried to his support.

"I SAID HE'S WITH US!" Siobhan reaffirmed, then, in French: "*IL EST PAN AM!*" And she bravely pushed the rifle aside so it was no longer pointing directly at me. Tough guts this class act who had grown up in the Bogside. I guess guns were nothing new to her.

"Show the pillow-biter your passport and I.D.," Bella suggested.

The soldier studied the documents for a moment, looking back and forth at them and me. He seemed confused.

"We have males with the airline now!" Siobhan said, with an air of complete authority. "We have *stewards*!"

The soldier looked me over once more and angrily thrust my passport and I.D. back at me. "You go!"

"Thanks," I whispered to Siobhan as we hurried through the checkpoint and my blood pressure dropped back below Frankenstein-lightning-bolt level. "What in God's name was happening to Beirut?"

29

New Delhi

It was the middle of the night when we made our final approach to New Delhi's Palam Airport, and we were all shocked to see the burned-out shell of a Lufthansa 707 lying at the edge of the airfield. The aircraft had crashed, skidded off the side of the runway and was engulfed in flames even before it had come to rest. The incident had occurred the day before and yet no one felt the urge to remove its gutted wreckage from the public eye. Not good advertisement for Lufthansa (where was the painter?) and not something any of us wanted to see just as we were dropping out of the sky about to touch down (the Lufthansa 707 remained there for such a long time, homeless locals eventually took up residence in an unscathed section of the fuselage…and the logo was finally painted over).

As our crew bus meandered through the empty countryside of the Union territories on its way to our hotel, I was haunted by the sight of the burned-out 707. We had learned in Training School that the materials from which aircraft interiors are made are highly flammable (consider this for a moment), but I didn't think I would ever see for myself, up close, the results of what had obviously been a raging inferno. I prayed that night that none of us would ever be involved in a fiery crash such as this. I didn't know it at the time, but my prayers would not be answered.

The rest of the crew were snoozing in the crew bus as it neared our hotel, but I wasn't the least bit tired. Once again, I was seeing and smelling my impressions of India. I say "smelling" because I believe that's what struck me the most, how different India smelt from my own country or my adopted country of England. It wasn't a bad smell and it wasn't a good smell. It was just a different smell. A dusty, smoky, sandalwood smell. On future trips to India, this common aroma would transform dramatically when the monsoons came, and the welcomed rains drenched the parched countryside and made it verdant and fragrant and soggy. Then your senses would be assaulted by a combination of floral wonders and a mixture of rotting fruit, diesel fumes and cow shit.

Thirty-minutes later, we pulled up in front of a red-and-white, corner-cupolaed, sandstone edifice, which more resembled a grand ornate Raj's palace than a layover hotel. It was the stunning Ashoka, one of the finest hotels in the country at that time (and the country's first government-owned hotel).

Previously, we had stayed at the Oberoi, which was distinctly captain's cabin, but not like this.

I jumped off the bus with the rest of the crew and went inside to a marble lobby tantalizingly oozing with Indian ambiance. It was hopelessly romantic. (The lobby was so vast, Delhi-ites would come here just to stroll, be seen and, perhaps just a little, to shelter and avoid the torrential downpours during the monsoon.)

Checking into hotels was usually quite simple and quite efficient. The hotel staff knew we were coming, and all we had to do was fill out a little registration card. One by one we received our keys and most shuffled off to catch some zees. I looked at my watch. It was coming up on four-thirty in the morning, and I still wasn't sleepy.

I was admiring chairs the size of thrones, glistening marble floors and uniformed employees sporting turbans, when I heard someone call: "Hey, Jon! Wanna have a beer?"

I looked round and saw Bernie our flight engineer waving a hand at me.

I checked my watch again. *A beer now?* is what I was thinking, but for some reason I said, "Let me just get out of my uniform…"

I ended up in the hotel bar with Bernie, the captain, and our first officer—all New York based. Bernie lived in Miami

Beach and commuted to New York, the captain commuted from Guadalajara to New York, and the first officer couldn't handle commuting, so he lived in Queens.

We sat in that bar for a long time and Bernie, the captain and the first officer did all the talking. I did all the listening. They were recounting airline stories.

They talked about how pilots got bored on long hauls. They talked about the captain who used to drink while he was on duty and even had to be taken off the airplane in a wheelchair so the passengers wouldn't notice that he was legless.

There was a story of a pilot who had a great sense of humour and thought it particularly hilarious to take a stroll back through the cabin during each flight. When he got right in the middle of the cabin he would drop a thick yellow book onto the carpet. He had printed up a fake title for the book. The book was entitled *HOW TO FLY A BOEING 747—for the Visually Impaired*.

And there was the one about the pilot who made a particularly hard landing in Hong Kong and the frisky stewardess who slid her pantyhose down around her ankles and burst into the cockpit, yelling: "You call that a landing!" Or the stewardess who convinced her captain to take off his uniform, trousers, hat and all, and then she put the entire captain's outfit on and strutted back through the cabin (while the captain sat in the cockpit in his balbriggans), hat flopping over her eyes, and trouser legs and coat sleeves drooping like a Raggedy Ann. Or the captain who thought it good fun to stumble back through the cabin probing and poking with a white cane (seriously!).

These are some of the stories I heard that night. And they made me laugh—and they made me think.

Finally the captain turned toward me. "We know it, but you're new, so you don't."

I just stared quietly back.

"In the airline business a pilot often 'fails upwards.'"

"Which means?" I asked.

"Which means that every once in a while someone ends up flying an airplane when they have no right to do so."

"And that means?"

"That means, don't ever fly with Captain Black. He has no business flying a 'seven-four.' He should never have been upgraded from 707s."

The skipper emptied his glass. "He's going to take a plane down with him one day."

This word of warning and the image of the burned-out Lufthansa aircraft haunted me that night.

30

Maiming Children

RING! RING! RING! I fumbled frantically for the telephone beside my bed.

"Hello?"

"Goood mor-neen Meeester Breakfeeelt. Eeet is ten o'clock. Time for you to be waking up."

"Thank you," I mumbled sleepily, wondering why I had asked for a ten o'clock wake-up.

I stared at the ceiling for a few moments while my pulse stabilized and the squirt of adrenal fluid dissipated. While I was looking at the ceiling, I realized I *hadn't* realized how elegant my hotel room was when I first arrived in India in the wee small hours. It was spacious beyond words, with high, coved ceilings. This was commonplace with the airline. We would fly to the backside of the planet and end up in an absolute palace.

I jumped in a gilt-edged shower, stared at a lion's head instead of a shower head and was pondering the rumour running around our airline that there was a cobra loose on the third floor of the hotel. I was on the second. The reason I was on the second floor was because one of my Training School classmate's father was a Pan Am captain and he had advised her to never stay higher than the second floor of a hotel, downline, in case of fire. Did that include snakes?

The phone rang again!

I stuck my head out of the shower curtain, and the ringing was right by my ear. There was a phone in the bathroom, as well.

"Hello?"

It was the same, friendly female voice: "Meeester Breakfeeelt, are you being awake?"

"Yes, I'm awake. Thank you. Why are you calling back?"

"Eeet is being service of hotel, Meeester Breakfeeelt. We always call back five minutes later to be asking 'Are you being awake?'"

I liked this personal touch. And the young lady with the silky voice was always there to wake me in the months to come as I had more flights to Delhi. I would receive the traditional wake-up call and then *the voice* would always call back exactly five minutes later when I was in the shower, "Meeester Breakfeeelt, are you being awake?"

What a lovely country, India, I decided.

I dressed and hurried downstairs. I was looking forward to today because I was meeting Bernie, and he was going to show me around Delhi. If you have a pen and paper, might I just tell you that Delhi is the capital of India and it's the third-largest city with a good ten million people. The city actually consists of two parts: Old Delhi and New Delhi, and they are divided by the Yamuna River. Old Delhi is the 17th-century walled city of Shahjahanabad with city gates, narrow alleys, the enormous Red Fort, temples, mosques and teeming bazaars.

Are you getting all this down?

New Delhi is a planned city of wide, tree-lined streets, parks and fountains. It was created by the British. Often flight crews are too exhausted to do much on a layover other than spend the entire time in bed sleeping, or otherwise, and since I wasn't tired and the otherwise was no more than a distant dream, I considered myself lucky to have someone like Bernie, who had been coming to India for ages, to give me a tour.

The cicadas whined in the distance and the sun bore down mercilessly as we hailed a taxi, of sorts, to take us to an area called Connaught Place in the center of Delhi. I say taxi, *of sorts*, because it was more of a motor-scooter powered rickshaw and as it noisily PUTT, PUTT, PUTTED away, I could feel the heat through the canvas top and smell the lack of hygiene from the driver.

Bernie turned to me: "Did you hear we're going to try to get back into Beirut?"

I was amazed. I didn't think I would ever get to see those

beautiful beaches again.

"That's the game plan for now, anyway. You know Pan Am—we will always go into a country to try to evacuate anybody who wants out."

After a very circuitous twenty minutes (avoiding sacred cows that were ambling unmolested right in the middle of traffic), our rickshaw motored into a district with major banks and airline offices, and we were there—Connaught Place. We tipped our driver a few rupees, and he sped off and joined a stream of other noisy motorized rickshaws polluting the air.

Connaught Place was among other things a bustling, quirky, dusty outdoor bazaar. We window-shopped from stall to stall and saw everything under the scorching sun for sale. As we passed lovely silk paintings and booksellers and sidewalk artists, I slowly realized we weren't alone. This was where I encountered my first beggar. And suddenly there were beggars everywhere, and these weren't just ordinary beggars, they had made a flourishing career out of it.

"Here comes the first one," Bernie warned, as an emaciated young woman, not unattractive but dressed in dirty shreds, made a move toward us. The woman was carrying a small baby.

"Look her baby's blind," I said. "I'm going to give her some rupees."

"Don't! She blinded the baby herself."

I couldn't believe what I was hearing.

"The baby wasn't born blind. They do it to heighten the pathos. They hope you'll give them more money. Some of these beggars make more money than senior civil servants."

"Bloody hell!"

The woman, who had savaged the eyes out of her own baby, clamped onto my arm and wouldn't let go. She reeked of uric acid and I tried to break loose, but she had a grip of steel. I told her firmly "No," and she held her baby up in front of my face so I could see its grossly ravaged eyes. But I kept walking and ignoring her and she eventually unclamped and went to importune a group of older German tourists.

I was flabbergasted. "I knew there'd be beggars, Bernie, but not butchers."

"It's not over yet. Here come some more."

Other beggars came up to us, holding babies who had some sort of deformity. "Look at these poor children."

"You're not going to want to hear this, but they maim their babies and break and twist the arms so their limbs are deformed. They want you to think it's some sort of ghoulish aberration of nature or their environment."

"I guess hunger drives people to act in ways beyond our wildest imagination," I said.

"Hunger and greed," Bernie said. "A 'begging mafia' controls many of these people. There's a slave trade where children, who are particularly compelling because of their disfigurement, and therefore effective beggars, are sold for huge sums."

We circled the square (not easy to circle a square), saw a man sprinkling cow urine in his hair, and then suddenly the number of beggars shadowing us grew rapidly. Most were small children and many were smiling and just curious because we looked so different.

"Just ignore them," is what Bernie told me, but I couldn't. When Bernie was looking the other way, I slipped some chewing gum to one of the smiling children. Better reinforce the smiling I thought than the butchering.

"What's the life expectancy here?"

"Not high, and I don't know how it works here in Delhi, but in Bombay I saw a tall lattice-work structure which looked like gigantic oven racks piled one on top of the other, called the Towers of Silence. They have workers whose sole job is to roam the city picking up dead bodies, of corresponding religion, mind you, and bring them to the Towers of Silence. Here they lay them out, row after row and level after level, thirty feet high and the vultures flock in droves and pick the corpses clean. When the vultures are finished with the dead there is nothing but bones remaining and the bones fall through the lattice structure and drop into a big pile at the bottom."

I walked on, wide-eyed, and now "Sahib! Sahib!" the cry came and the beggars seemed to be multiplying exponentially.

"Let's get out of here," Bernie said. "Let's go over to the Oberoi Hotel and go for a swim."

"I could just go for a swim, it must be over a hundred today."

"Try over a hundred and ten."

But we didn't go swimming when we got to the Oberoi. In fact we didn't even want to go near the water. The water in the swimming pool was a brown, murky cesspool. It looked like a swamp—without the crocodiles.

We moved two lounge chairs into the shade of a cypress tree and plopped down. I sat back in my lounge chair and my eye caught something up on the roof of the hotel. "Uh, oh, Bernie, look. Friends of yours?"

Up on the roof, hunched over and staring morosely down at us, was a small group of vultures.

"India's version of flying rats. They'll eat anything."

The temperature was soaring, so we decided to stay put and have some lunch. Right off I noticed two things on the menu which seemed wildly out of place in India—hamburgers and Wiener Schnitzel.

"I'm going to go for the Wiener Schnitzel. This I've got to try. How can they possibly sell Wiener Schnitzel in Delhi?"

"I don't know if I would risk it if I were you."

"C'mon, Bernie. You only live once."

"That's precisely my point. Haven't you heard of 'Delhi Belly?'"

"Food poisoning, right?"

"Major league food poisoning. It's trying to kill you and you're wishing you were dead. You're both shooting for the same goal."

"I'm still going to give it a try. What about you?"

"Think I'll just have a beer."

My schnitzel arrived, and I was surprised that it looked exactly like the tasty schnitzels I had consumed on many occasions in Austria.

"See, Bernie, look at this lovely little piece of breaded veal."

"We're in India, Jon, can't be veal."

"Geez, hope it's not monkey, or something worse."

"What's worse than monkey?"

I took my knife and fork and attempted a nice incision, but the knife wouldn't go in and just the breaded layer sloughed off exposing some hideous, blue, bulbous mass. "My God, look at the colour of this."

Bernie just rolled back in his chair, laughing.

We sat there in silence for a while enjoying the relaxing atmosphere and two Swissair hostesses in flattering bikinis.

"So whaddaya think's happening back in Beirut, Bernie?"

"We'll find out soon enough. Now forget about Lebanon, I'm concentrating on Switzerland."

I saw the waiter coming, so I quickly dumped my schnitzel in a nearby garbage bin.

"Hi. Could I order a hamburger now, please? I'm famished today."

"This I am already knowing," said the waiter in the staccato delivery the Indians have. "One hamburger be coming right up."

Bernie ordered another beer and just a few moments later the brewski arrived accompanied by something vaguely resembling a hamburger. I bit into the beast and immediately realized any resemblance to a hamburger, in the Western world, stopped with its appearance. But at least it wasn't blue inside.

I remember Bernie lapping at his beer and dreamily saying something rude about the Swissair hostesses, when there was a tremendous rush of air and someone slapped me hard across the face and stole my hamburger.

Beggars! But, no, taking off with my lunch was one of the resident hotel vultures. I looked over at Bernie.

"That," he said, "is one smart bird. Even he waited until you dumped the schnitzel."

31

Do Not Attempt to Land!

We were delayed departing Delhi and we experienced the uncommon joy of boarding the aircraft and getting it ready when it was daylight, albeit, just after dawn.

As I moved to the aft section, to my assigned position at R5, I was stunned to see about five or six rows on the starboard side blocked off with a white curtain? What was behind the curtain? There had been no mention about this during our briefing.

Should I split the curtains and peek inside?

What would you do?

I peeked.

"Hello," came a weak voice.

This area had been transformed into a hospital bed. The window shades were down, and a heavy-set older gentleman was staring back at me.

"Hi, my name's Jon. I'll be working this section...and I'll be looking after you. Can I get you anything?"

The older gentleman shook his head "No," then proceeded to tell me that he had been on Indian Airlines flight 440, a domestic flight from Madras to Delhi, and it had crashed on landing and began burning. He had been sitting a few rows in front of an over-wing exit and had escaped out of the aircraft and out onto the wing. And he jumped, but he was so heavy he didn't jump far enough and broke his back on the wing on the way down. He lay under the burning airplane thinking about his grandchildren, figuring his number was up, when he was finally pulled to safety.

And now he was on his way home.

"I'll take good care of you," I said. "Do you want to sleep or do you want me to bug you?"

"Sleep," he said. "But you can bug me later." And despite all he had been through, he managed a smile.

As we climbed to our cruising altitude, a voice came over the intercom from the cockpit. "Ladies and gentlemen, if you look out the right side of the aircraft, you can see quite a breathtaking sight in the distance—Mount Everest!"

I undid my shoulder harness and went up to my new friend behind the curtain. I peeped in. He was awake. He had his head turned but couldn't look out the window. I lifted the shade closest to his head and he looked out in the direction of Mt. Everest.

"Which one is it?" he asked.

"There," I said, now realizing that there are a whole bunch of high peaks you see from up here. "See what looks like cat's ears? The right ear is cut off at the top. That's Lhotse. The left ear is Everest. Want me to close the shade?"

"Leave it open, please."

Also in my section this day, seated in the front row by R4, were two seriously sunburned British lads who had just climbed Mt. Everest and now they were on their way home, back to the UK. The two British climbers told me in detail of their treacherous climb to the summit and it almost made we want to have a go myself.

Almost.

Perhaps better to see it from up here.

* * *

"Do not attempt to land in Beirut! Repeat. Do not attempt to land. WE CAN NOT GUARANTEE YOUR SAFETY!"

This is what the cockpit heard coming in over our aircraft's radio. Close call. We had already started our descent into Beirut when we learned that sporadic fighting had broken out.

The captain banked the jumbo sharply, and we climbed steadily, heading away from the burgeoning conflict. I wondered if I would ever see Beirut again—as she had been—a charismatic blend of the Middle East and Europe. Civil war was about to ruin what had been a very civil city.

Later, I would learn there's always more to war than meets the eye. While the Shiites and Sunnis and Maronites were all fighting each other, killing off men, women and children, behind the scenes they were cooperating in drug trafficking.

Money and drugs reigned supreme over war and ethnic hatred.

32

A Delicate Situation

When I woke up I didn't know where I was—all I knew was that I was in an incredible amount of pain. Little pitchforks jabbed in the back of my eyeballs, an air-hammer pounded away at the base of my skull, and my stomach was cramped so severely I was frozen in an alarmingly familiar prenatal curl.

What the hell had happened? Where was I?

The door to the room I was in opened and a dark figure appeared in the doorway brandishing what looked like a weapon. The dark figure raised the weapon to finish me off, but I couldn't do anything about it. I couldn't run, I couldn't even yell for help, all I could do was lie there helplessly and moan.

"Lucozade," said the dark figure. "Drink it. It will make you feel better." A light switched on, and I saw my roommate Vigdis standing there. "Is there anything else I can do for you?"

"Can you turn off the light, please?" The light made the shooting pain behind my eyes feel as if someone had plugged my eyes into a wall socket.

"You have Delhi Belly."

"But I didn't get a chance to eat any of my food in Delhi."

"Did you even take a bite of anything?"

"Hamburger…"

"That'll do it. I'll let you sleep now."

Vigdis pulled the door shut and I closed my eyes, then they shot back open. I crawled out of bed and tried to get to the loo. It was an explosive situation and I was nearing Kaopectate Alert Level 10.

"Vigdis!"

I crept down the hall like a man carrying nitroglycerin. I

stopped in front of the bathroom door too weak to even open the door. I pointed at it with a shaky finger. "Vigdis!"

Vigdis hurried to my aid and tried the door, but it wouldn't open. She tried it again. Nothing. The molten lava deep within was threatening to erupt like Kilauea.

"HURR-RY!"

"It's locked," Vigdis said. "I guess Sarah's in there."

"Sarah? SARAH?!!! I was suddenly lucid. "SHE'S STILL HERE? WHAT'S SHE STILL DOING HERE? I'LL KILL HER!!!"

"Quiet, she'll hear you."

"I WANT HER TO HEAR ME!!!" I screamed, then went limp again.

We waited an agonizingly long time. Nearly too long, might I add. Close, but no cigar. Finally the door opened and out came a cloud of sickening Giorgio perfume. Somewhere in the middle of the Giorgio was Sarah.

"Hi! I've got a date!" Sarah, announced with great bravado. "Catcha later."

I lunged at her as she passed by, but I wasn't quick enough to grab her by the throat. She was already out the door and gone.

When I eventually crawled from the loo, I berated Sarah in absentia until I couldn't go on anymore.

"Come along, Jon, we must get you back to bed. You look even worse—if that's possible."

Vigdis got me tucked into bed again. "I have a New York, today. Must be going soon."

"But...but..."

"Don't worry, Wendy is due back from Hamburg this evening. If you're still alive, she'll take over. Australians have lots of experience dealing with vomit."

Vigdis slipped out of the room and left me to my gloom.

"Vigdis?" I moaned.

The door opened a crack. "What is it?"

"I have to go to the loo again. Hurry!"

It took me another 24 hours to recover from my food

poisoning, and when I awoke to a sunny morning without the splitting pain behind my eyeballs, I knew I was well on the road to recovery.

I was lounging in bed, gazing out the window at the glorious occurrence of sun in London, when I heard clinking noises coming from the kitchen. I sat up in bed and decided that even though I felt weak I was in need of some fluid.

"Good morning," I said to my flatmate Wendy. "I'm alive."

"You look no worse for wear. Only thinner."

"Must've lost a stone. Don't recommend the weight-loss regime."

Wendy had a funny look on her face. "I have good news and bad news."

"Don't tell me. Let me guess. The bad news involves Sarah."

"No, the bad news involves Rob. He's going to base-trade to San Francisco."

This I was sad to learn. Rob was the quintessential roommate.

"And the good news?"

"Sarah left just before you came to."

"She finally left?" I asked incredulously. "Did she leave money for the phone?"

"No. She didn't even say thank you. I've never seen a woman like that, but in your own way I think you paid her back."

"How so?"

"Remember she went out on a date?"

I nodded.

"Well, her date took her out for a curry. To a restaurant called the Taj of Piccadilly.

"The Indian restaurant with the Bangladeshi waiters?"

"That's the one. And guess what? Sarah ate something that didn't agree with her."

"She got Delhi Belly in London?"

"She spent all last night and this morning on the toilet."

"Well, justice has been served. I'm sorry she put everyone out like that."

"What are you going to do now that you're back among the living?"

"I think I'm going to take a hot bath and go die in bed again. Catch up on all the sleep I couldn't catch up on when I lay there moaning."

I dragged myself off to the bathroom, beaten by the bug and beaten by inconsiderate humanity. I ran steaming water and immersed myself, trying to let my repulsion for Sarah dissipate in the bubbly bath. And you know what? It worked. Things weren't so bad after all. Maybe I had been too hard on Sarah. Poor thing. She had had a run of bad luck, so to speak. When I had enough of lolling in the tub, I stood up and reached for my nice fluffy bath towel.

Poised like a deadly viper, on top of my nice clean cotton towel, was a pair of Sarah's discarded panty hose—a monument and heavily loaded testimony of her explosive bout with London curry.

I know, I know, revolting to you, dear reader, but believe me that pales in comparison to how revolting it was to me that fragile morning back in London.

"Where on earth are you going?" Wendy queried, as I struggled out the front door of our flat. "I thought you were going back to bed."

I held up a bulging manila envelope: "I have to post this."

"Can't it wait?"

"No, it can't wait. Sarah forgot something. A souvenir. I'm going to mail it to her. At the bank. Signature required."

33

A Good Night for a Ditching

It was months later, and we were on our way back to London from New York. We were a Pan Am cockpit and cabin crew operating a Delta Airlines 747. This occurred occasionally. Having said that, it hadn't been mentioned to us during our briefing, and we were all just a bit stunned as we walked through the jet-bridge and saw the Delta logo emblazoned on the side of the aircraft.

It had been great to be back in the city that never sleeps, where cozy restaurants with spirited owners posted whimsical signs, such as: "There's no place like this place near this place, so this must be the place."

I had run into some of my old classmates, like Ruth and Carrie Thomas, and we had lunch at a pub called "The Pub." The Pub, located on the Upper West Side, skirted a colourful gay enclave shamelessly coined the "Swish Alps."

My good friends were all flying to exotic locales now, and it was particularly exciting for Carrie, who had grown up in New York, and now was based in New York, to be enjoying such far-flung experiences beyond her original horizons.

"I can't even believe it. Three days ago I was shopping in Milan and staring at the most gorgeous men in the world, and tomorrow I'm going to Rio where I hear they're even more desirable."

This is what I was thinking about, Carrie and her *joie de vivre*, when I felt the first vibrations.

"Ladies and gentlemen," came a southern drawl over the intercom. It was the dead middle of the night and the captain's rural voice woke everybody up. "This here's yer capt'n speakin'. We're presently experiencin' just a pesky little mechanical difficulty with owa numba fo-wa ingin. Y'all may feel a little vibration, but it's nothin' ta be concerned with. This will not affect owa present altitude of thirty-eight thousand feet and wea still projectin' an on-tahm arrival in London. Ah'll be keepin' y'all posted on any and all developments."

The captain's voice had sounded calm but, nevertheless, it had sent icy shivers through us all. When you are only halfway across the Atlantic, you are hours from anything resembling Sweet Home terra firma.

I was lucky enough to be flying with Siobhan and Bella again, so I immediately went up to First Class. They were just descending the spiral staircase.

"What's the real story?" I whispered, as Siobhan ushered me into the First-Class galley.

"They're hoping like hell we don't lose any more power in that engine."

"And if we do?"

"Let's not even think about it."

I went about my business for the next half an hour, but I was a coiled spring inside. I knew it was half an hour later because I kept looking at my watch.

"This here's the capt'n speakin' agin." He sounded unnaturally calm. "Ah have an update for y'all…"

This was the first time I observed all the passengers in an airplane pay attention to an announcement.

"We're gonna hav' ta shut down that numba fo-wa ingin…"

Quiet as a morgue.

"…but ah want y'all ta know, these 747s are built so they can fly as well on three ingins as on fo-wa."

This, myself, I was having a tough time buying. If they could fly as well on three, as on four, why didn't they just build the bloody things that way, put two engines on the left wing and one on the right.

The captain went on: "Ah want to assure y'all that we will have no trouble maintainin' owa present altitude and reachin' owa destination. Ah'll be checkin' in with y'all from tahm ta tahm ta give ya any further information."

There was an odd tension in the cabin. In spite of the darkness, everyone tried to look out the window to see the ill-fated engine (passengers were asking me, "Which one's number four?").

Siobhan walked through the cabin smiling her reassuring smile at everybody, exuding inner strength, greeting each of the passengers individually like the Duchess of Kent greets the ball boys and ball girls at Wimbledon. This had a remarkably soothing effect on everyone, including myself.

Then we heard the captain's voice again. "This here's the capt'n, ah'm afraid we've started ta lose powa in a second ingin..." Everyone in the cabin froze. "...and this is gonna slow us down a bit (no shit). We're still plannin' on makin' Heathrow with no problem although this loss of powa in the numba two ingin will reduce owa air speed. So, for ya own safety ah'm gonna instruct the cabin crew ta pass through the cabin now and review the "water landing" procedure with y'all. Remember, this is just a precaution."

Well needless to say passengers don't like hearing "water landing," precaution or not. As we passed through the cabin to review emergency procedures, like donning of life vests and evacuation of the aircraft, I looked into many terrified eyes.

The aircraft droned on in this manner for an eternity, which was good, for we thought we had really covered some distance, but in reality it might have only been an hour (we still had two more hours to go). There was a full moon out now, and most passengers seated near the windows spent a lot of time peering out. And down, to see if they could see the ocean.

Once again, I nonchalantly strolled up to First Class to talk to Siobhan. She was just coming down the spiral staircase again. Without speaking she grabbed Bella and we all sidled over to the privacy of the galley. Siobhan's face was grim. "That second engine, he may have to shut it down."

I could feel my stomach lurch.

"We're going to start losing altitude?" Bella asked.

Siobhan leaned close. "After the first engine went, we descended to 8,000 feet, now we've slowly been losing altitude for the last hour already."

"What's the game plan?" Bella asked.

"The game plan is we pray we can make landfall in Ireland. If not, we're going swimming."

I went into one of the lavatories, locked myself in and looked in the mirror. Jesus, this just can't be true. We have over three hundred people onboard. We have babies onboard. I stared in the mirror for a moment longer and then looked around the confined lavatory. A wave of claustrophobia swept over me. God help us! I threw some water on my face, dried off and returned to the cabin.

There were so many worried faces out there, and they were following our every move. We represented their link to getting through this nightmare alive. Couples, young and old, held hands, babies were cradled and rocked, strangers conversed and formed desperate bonds. I wondered how many of us would get out alive if the plane did go down.

My mind flashed back to "THE FILM" in Training School. The one about the plane ditching in the Pacific between San Francisco and Honolulu.

With this image forefront in my mind, I went up to First Class and asked Siobhan if the captain knew if there were any ships in the vicinity.

"No, Jon. I've already asked. We're out here all by ourselves."

And then the announcement came: "Good mornin' ladies and gentlemen. This here's the capt'n agin. Looks like wea gonna hav' ta shut down that second ingin. While we won't be able ta maintain owa original altitude, we should have no trouble reachin' the coast of Ireland and now wea projectin' ta land at Shannon in just over an hour."

In spite of the captain's "up delivery" the situation had clearly worsened, and the passengers sensed it. Immediately a remarkable number of people needed to visit the lavatories.

Then it must have been no more than five minutes later when we hit some turbulence and this sent sizzling lightning bolts through the passengers' raw nerve endings. Everyone onboard wondered how a limping aircraft could possibly have a chance in turbulence.

Many passengers had their headsets on, listening to music, trying to make the time go by faster, trying to take their mind off the serious situation. When their music abruptly ceased and they heard the soft hum which meant the captain was breaking in to make an announcement, I saw half the cabin physically jump like a shoal of fish jump when you throw a stone into the water.

"This here's your capt'n..." And his voice was somber now. "We're losin' powa in a third ingin and it doesn't look like we're gonna make the Irish coast..."

Frightened gasps in the cabin.

"...there's a full moon and the seas are calm...so from that aspect...we couldn't ask for better conditions ta attempt a water landing..."

Near panic in the cabin.

"...at this tahm ah'm gonna ask the cabin crew ta pass through the aisles and secure the aircraft. Meanwhile, rest assured that the three of us up here on the flight deck will do owa best ta get the aircraft as close ta the coast as we can."

My heart pounded. Something every one of us who had ever flown over water had thought about, was happening. Ugly images rushed through my brain: blackness, ice-cold water, trapped inside a sinking aircraft, claustrophobia, sharks. Oh, dear God, please let me wake up and be back in my bed in London.

Other images rushed through my mind. Images of my family, my friends, a high school football game, an autumn day in Wisconsin—a young boy with his older brother skipping stones on Lake Michigan.

My mind was racing when Siobhan made her announcement: "Ladies and gentlemen, this is your In-flight Director. The flight attendants will be passing through the cabin to collect any loose objects that are in the area around your seats. We also need to collect all shoes and other loose objects such as pens, eye glasses and false teeth."

And this emergency measure caused near anarchy. "Please," implored an older Eastern European couple, "don't make us give up our false teeth. Please."

"But I have to," I whispered to them. "Please understand. I have to stow them. If we hit the water hard, they'll fly through the cabin like they've been shot out of a cannon."

The older woman began to cry. "Please. Please, don't take away our dignity."

Dignity, the word leapt out and screamed in my brain. I had learned something about dignity from a friend once back in the Basque Country. But I didn't understand why giving up their false teeth was so important to this elderly couple—until I saw that the older man was wearing a yarmulke.

"Come with me," I motioned to the two of them. "Move up here by the bulkhead. In this row there's nobody in front of you, only this wall. Here you can keep your teeth."

And then there were the babies. We had learned in Training School that "babies simply don't survive crashes." We had to make sure the parents weren't putting the baby on the inside of their own seatbelts. That would crush the baby on impact. We had to show panicked parents a special way to hold their baby. That was their only hope. In fact, we knew damn well that the minute the plane hit the water, if a crushing impact came, the baby would rocket from the parent's arms no matter how tightly it was being held. If false teeth could be wrenched from its owner's mouth with jaws clenched tight and become a deadly projectile, you can well imagine what would happen to a small infant.

There was no time to neatly place or carefully pack the pens, eye glasses, false teeth, books, shoes, and other possible projectiles that these dear passengers gave us. They were just dumped on the floor of the toilets. Then we started piling on top the larger items which were loose in the cabin. Baby bottles, briefcases, and even women's expensive fur coats were thrown right in with debris from the galley such as uneaten meals, cakes and desserts. Then the doors to the toilets were sealed.

Now the time had come to demonstrate the "brace position" for impact. And we told the passengers the real reason for not inflating their vests inside the airplane.

"If you inflate your vest inside the aircraft and the plane is sinking, you will become a bobbing cork trapped inside. You will never be able to swim underwater to safety with an inflated vest."

When the preparation for the ditching was completed, I returned to my jump seat and took a quick glance out the window. What I saw outside made me feel as if someone had hit my stomach with an axe. Down below, in the light of the full moon, I could see the water, and the water wasn't all that far away.

This was it. The time had come. I hoped like hell we were ready.

"Ladies and gentlemen, this is yer capt'n agin. When ya hear the command 'BRACE!' Ah want y'all ta brace yourselves as you've been shown and stay that way until we have come to a complete stop and we issue the command ta evacuate the aircraft."

Most passengers braced themselves right then and there.

Siobhan dimmed the cabin lights (just the hint of dawn was begrudgingly visible as a bloody smear in the east). On regular flights, we always announced that the cabin lights were being dimmed on landing so the passengers could enjoy the arrival into a city, but the real reason was in case of an accident. If there was an emergency, the crew's eyes would be accustomed to the blackness that would come with the crash.

A long moment passed. Another moment. Why wasn't the captain yelling "Brace?" Each second was an ice age. Each small noise shot a million watts through me. In any moment our aircraft would cease being a flying machine and would become a deadly out of control object, skipping crazily along the cement surface of the ocean. An ocean of cold, deep, black water. Where was that command? The last seconds were unbearable.

A tremendous ROAR.

Adrenaline spurted red-hot through my body. My heart pounded a hole in my chest. My eyes were wide, like an animal's. I saw everything in slow motion…

…and that's when I realized the roar wasn't from any impact, and it wasn't from any crash, rather it was from the passengers. I jammed myself forward in my jump seat and strained to get a look out the window at my exit, and oh my dear God, we were just skimming over the emerald coast of Ireland. Thank you, God. Thank you for that beautiful Irish coast. We had made land.

And the twenty miles in to Shannon Airport.

* * *

Once we had landed, blocked and shut down the engines, we had the unenviable task of returning all the items we had thrown unceremoniously into the lavatories. When it was all over and all personal items had been returned to the passengers, we had just one item remaining—a man's left shoe. Why was there only one shoe?

We made an announcement.

No one responded.

We made the announcement again.

Finally a call button pinged on. The shoe was returned. The man grateful, yet oddly sheepish.

He had but one leg.

34

Not Allowed to Project Fatigue

We were flying London to L.A. When we were three hours out, the captain advised us that owing to uncharacteristically strong headwinds, we would have to divert to Winnipeg to refuel.

We landed safely at Winnipeg International, taxied to a holding area and waited for the fuel truck.

I watched out a window as the fuel truck arrived, did its thing, but didn't depart. Half an hour elapsed and he still hadn't budged. What was going on?

Eventually, Corolla came down the spiral staircase. "For the love of God, we can't start up until we pay!"

My mind flashed back to Susan Lovejoy in Angola. *Wait! This was not the Third World, this was Canada! Our good, hockey-loving neighbour! How could this be?*

I told Corolla about Susan Lovejoy and her colleagues passing the hat.

"Bless you, laddie, let me go tell the captain," and she scurried back up the spiral staircase.

Corolla was gone for a long time. Everyone was growing restless. Everyone was tired. Announcements were made to tame the passengers. When Corolla eventually appeared on the spiral staircase again, she was laughing.

"You won't believe it!" she whispered, ushering me over by the galley. "No need to pass the hat. The first officer put it all on his Chevron Gold credit card!"

I was speechless.

Corolla went on: "Can you imagine when some poor Chevron employee dutifully prepares the first officer's monthly statement back at Chevron headquarters? 'Ah, let's see here: ten dollars at Duke's Chevron in Santa Monica ... twelve dollars at Sammie's Sepulveda Chevron ... and $25,000 at the Winnipeg International Airport!'"

We were exhausted by the time we made it to our layover hotel, and were still exhausted the next day as we prepared for our flight back to London Heathrow. At least it would be a zippy flight back home, those headwinds would now be tailwinds and they were still raging.

The flight was scheduled to take 10½ hours, and we would be able to "go over the pole" in a lot less than that.

We departed Los Angeles on time and took off over the beach at El Segundo into a setting sun. I was seated at R5. As I've mentioned before, I loved working the back of the bus as I could look all the way up through economy and watch the goings on. When we had turbulence, I could see the fuselage gently twist. And as many of you know, back in the aft section of the aircraft you feel the turbulence more, sort of a dog wagging its tail.

It was something most of us became accustomed to.

We survived the drinks service, the dinner service, and then we dimmed the lights and started the movie. All the screens behaved and descended as they should, and all the projectors actually functioned and didn't melt down (no personal back-of-the-seat screens in those days).

We flew through the night and I remember walking through the cabin offering orange juice and water to absolutely no one. Everyone was sleeping. Some snoring. Some making rude noises. No babies crying. Seatbelts fastened over the blankets so we could check them. Clipper socks donned. Eye shades in place.

It was a picture postcard crossing.

Most of my colleagues took a break and had a little nap, but I didn't. I hung out in the back galley and chatted with whomever was awake.

A few hours later, we turned up the cabin lights to start the breakfast service. It went without a hitch. We served seconds on coffee and tea, and passengers soon flocked to the lavatories.

After we cleared the cabin, I went to my jump seat and peered out and down below as we crossed over the Irish coast (always remembering that close call) and then the west coast of England. This was always my favourite part of the trip: it was still pitch black out, no light in the sky, but I could see the glow from the sodium lights twinkling in all the little storybook villages.

As we crossed over Cornwall and Devon, my view of the twinkling lights was blocked by an annoying ground fog.

During our descent into Heathrow, the captain made an announcement: "Good morning, ladies and gentlemen, there's a fair amount of fog this morning and we're going to hold until it clears."

London...Fog...No surprise.

We circled for an hour.

It was getting light.

We circled some more.

Through the odd break in the fog, I could make out the Thames far below.

Then the captain came on again: "The fog is not lifting so we're going to divert to Paris. We'll refuel and the minute London opens back up, we'll be in the air and back on our way."

We flew to Paris but were placed in a holding pattern thanks to the many other diverted flights.

Eventually, we touched down at Aéroport Roissy-Charles de Gaulle, and were directed to an area of the airport where there were no jet bridges. We shut down the engines. No one was allowed to leave the aircraft.

We served orange juice and water to our passengers.

And we waited.

And we waited...

We waited for *eight* hours.

And we ran out of orange juice and water and anything to eat.

Even the peanuts.

It was stiflingly hot on the aircraft and we were all

uncomfortable. Our passengers, who had been well behaved up until now, started to grumble. We tried to keep the passengers in the loop and informed. We did this through numerous announcements and staying visible. Easy to be annoyed with a disembodied voice coming over the intercom, less so with a smiley face at your seat.

We were getting more and more tired now, but as flight attendants we weren't allowed to "project fatigue." That essentially meant that we couldn't say "in two hours I'm going to be shattered and unable to perform my duties."

The reason I mention this is, by union mandate, we were allowed to walk off the aircraft if we had gone over our duty day.

And now we were *all* over our duty day.

Eight of our fellow flight attendants bolted, leaving us in a bit of a lurch. They were taken to a hotel where they could eat, drink, sleep.

There were now ten of us left in the cabin. If I can remember correctly, I think Pan Am rules stated that there had to be a minimum of 12 cabin attendants, but the FAA would let you fly with ten if ALL EXITS were manned.

It was early evening when London opened back up. We were finally able to start up the engines and get some A/C in the cabin. Imminent departure always gives you a shot of adrenaline and with an end to this marathon in sight, the passengers re-found their sense of humour.

We took off and flew the fifty-two minutes to London. And were immediately put in a holding pattern. Everyone wanted back in and we weren't the first.

We held.

And we held.

Finally given the clearance to land.

And the fog came back.

We held for another two hours, circling. And I fell asleep sitting at my jump seat. I remember a young German girl playfully punching me and telling me to "*Wach auf!*"

I spoke to the young girl for a while and it was about the time I saw London down below, that the announcement was made that we had been cleared to land. I got the young girl back to her seat and strapped in. We landed with the sun setting.

It was Thanksgiving Day.

Our "flight time" from L.A. to London: 23½ hours.

And our skeleton cabin crew of ten weary, yet intrepid-and-proud souls, ended up being awarded Employees of the Month for that October back in 1973.

35

The Worst News Possible

I was in San Francisco on a layover, marvelling as the fog did the cat's paw thing across the bay toward Alcatraz, when my phone rang.

"It's Stan Oliver, Jon."

"Hey, Stanford!"

"Are you sitting down?"

I could tell by the tone of my former classmate's voice that something was desperately wrong. "Yes," I said, even though I wasn't. "What's up?"

"There's been a horrific accident. A KLM 747 was trying to take off when it hit one of our 747s taxing on the runway in the Canary Islands. It was foggy. There were explosions. Carrie was working the flight."

My heart jammed up into my throat. "Is she okay?"

"She didn't make it."

I couldn't speak. Carrie Thomas dead? *Jesus.* I don't remember Stan saying anything else to me. I don't even remember hanging up the phone. But I do remember, and I will never forget, classmate, friend and most remarkable young lady, Carol "Carrie" Thomas, taken from us on that foggy runway in Tenerife.

Later I was to find out what had happened. Here is the sequence of events:

Two jumbos were heading for the popular tourist destination of Las Palmas on the island of Gran Canaria, one of the Canary Islands, 93 miles off the west coast of North Africa. One, a Pan Am charter flight, was coming in from Los Angeles. It had transited New York to pick up 14 passengers, change crew, refuel, then it had flown through the night. The other, a Royal Dutch Airlines, was coming in from

Amsterdam. There were a total of 644 passengers between the two 747s.

Just before the two aircraft were to land at the airport in Las Palmas, Gran Canaria, separatists, called *Fuerzas Arnadas Guanches*, who wanted Canary Island independence from Spain, exploded a bomb in the flower shop on the terminal concourse. Eight people were injured, one seriously. Later, another telephone call was received claiming responsibility for the explosion and hinting that a second bomb had been planted somewhere in the terminal building. Civil aviation authorities had no choice but to close the airport pending a thorough search for the second bomb. The closure necessitated the diversion of all incoming flights to the nearby island of Tenerife.

Pan Am requested to hold and circle. They had enough fuel for two more hours. Oddly, the request was denied, and they, too, were forced to head to Tenerife and its much smaller airport at Los Rodeos.

Los Rodeos rests at 2,073 feet, in a rugged swale between two extinct volcanoes. It's one of the most dangerous airports in the world, and pilots do not like coming in here. The airport is just a few miles from the coast. The weather is wildly mercurial. When thick clouds roll in, they produce rapid and drastic changes in visibility and temperature. One minute it's sunny, the next minute you can't see your hand in front of your face.

There was only one landing strip, many runway lights were out of order, including all the center lights, and the runway/taxiway intersections were not lit or properly marked.

Pan Am Clipper *Victor* landed safely and taxied to an area at the end of the taxiway. As more and more planes landed, the airport quickly became choked with diverted flights. Airlines were suddenly behind schedule and crews were afraid their duty time would be exceeded. In the case of KLM, it didn't just mean getting back to home base in Amsterdam too late to have legal rest before they were due to take their next trip, it meant losing their job, their career, being *prosecuted under Dutch law*. How do you perform with that kind of stress hanging over your head? Pressure was on the pilots. A gigantic domino effect was about to come thundering down.

It was Sunday afternoon. There were only two Air Traffic Controllers on duty at the normally backwater Tenerife airport, and they were floundering in bilingual stress. One ATC handled arrivals and departures, the other ATC dealt with ground control. There was no ground radar.

The Air Traffic Controllers wanted everyone the hell out, *and soon*, there were more pressing concerns: There was a football game on the radio, a friendly between Spain and Hungary.

Passengers were allowed to disembark from KLM and they all filed into an overcrowded terminal. Pan Am only allowed its passengers down onto the tarmac, so they could stretch their legs and, more importantly, be easily rounded up when Pan Am was given start-up clearance.

In the cockpits, crew were waiting. Itching to leave. Growing impatient. Nobody wanted to be stranded overnight. Airlines are not keen on the unwanted expenses and logistics of putting up hundreds of passengers. And don't forget the food vouchers.

Then Mother Nature had a mood swing, the weather began to deteriorate, and clouds hanging over the hills to the south began to cascade down those hills and creep menacingly toward the airport.

On the ground, the KLM captain made the fatal decision to refuel so he wouldn't lose yet more time when he got back into Las Palmas. KLM began taking on 55,000 additional liters of fuel. If KLM hadn't chosen to refuel, everyone could have gone on their way before the airport became socked in.

Pan Am's Captain Victor Grubbs had an idea, even though KLM was blocking their way, perhaps there was just enough room to squeeze by the refueling jumbo?

First Officer Robert Bragg and Flight Engineer George Warns went down to the tarmac and stepped off the distance between Pan Am's wingtip and KLM's wingtip in the hope of

Pan Am being able to taxi around the refueling KLM jumbo. They were 12 feet too short.

Pan Am was stuck behind KLM.

Yet another proverbial nail in the coffin.

An announcement was made in the terminal. The airport in Las Palmas had reopened. Two aircraft sitting ahead of KLM and Pan Am departed safely into 15-plus visibility.

Pan Am quickly re-boarded its passengers. Passengers returned to KLM, but there were problems: A Dutch couple realized their children were missing and this caused a further delay.

TICK. TICK. TICK. The clouds crept farther down the neighbouring hills.

One passenger on KLM chose to stay behind against airline and airport rules. She was a Dutch tour guide by the name of Robina Van Lanschot. She didn't re-board as she lived in nearby Puerto de la Cruz, and wanted to get back home to be with her boyfriend. She wanted to avoid flying back to Gran Canaria, only to have to get on another flight to come right back to Tenerife.

This decision would save her life.

Finally, the control tower gave KLM permission to taxi, followed by Pan Am. They were both "backtracking" or "back-taxiing" (going upstream) on that one and only runway. KLM was first. Pan Am second. KLM was supposed to go to the end of the runway, turn around, and hold for clearance. Pan Am had been instructed to follow KLM, but only as far as the *third* turn-off, then exit the "active" and hold there safely out of the way until KLM was airborne.

The clouds on the hills to the right of the airport continued to misbehave and encroached onto the runway. There was now pea-soup fog and it was spitting. Visibility dropped below a hundred meters. Then it dropper further. Pan Am could only crawl along the runway at 3 knots. With the drizzle and the fog, there was so much moisture in the air, windscreen wipers had to be used to see out of the cockpit.

The Pan Am crew had now been on duty for 11¼ hours.

KLM 9¼.

Because of heavy Spanish accents, both crews were having trouble understanding instructions from the control tower.

Pan Am taxied right on past the third turn-off because it didn't appear to be a proper turnoff as it was a near hairpin 135-degree turn to the left. On the Los Rodeos airport diagram, this exit is shown as C-3, but Pan Am's chart did not designate the exits by letter and number. There were no signs or other markings identifying the runway exits, so Pan Am continued on down the active runway looking for a turn-off that more resembled a proper taxiway.

My question is: Why was Pan Am instructed to turn off at C-3? The smaller aircraft that had just taken off before KLM had been allowed to take the more amenable and safer C-4.

The temperature was 14C.

The dew point 13C.

A meteorological boiling cauldron.

On account of the thick fog, Pan Am couldn't see the KLM 747 at the other end of the runway turn around and face them.

There was confusion in both cockpits. There was confusion between KLM and the tower. Then Pan Am and the control tower transmitted at the same time. They both spoke over each other. The simultaneous radio transmissions coming into the KLM flight deck caused distortion and was heard as a piercing, three-second squeal.

Confusion and uncertainty, yet the KLM 747 was already accelerating down the runway at 160 miles-per-hour and right at Pan Am. Pan Am still couldn't see KLM bearing down on them but sensed something was desperately wrong.

Here's a transcript of an audio clip from the Pan Am flight deck:

Captain: *"Let's get the hell out of here."*

First Officer: *"Yeah, he's anxious, isn't he."* (referring to KLM)

Flight Engineer: *"Yeah, after he held us up for an hour and a half…now he's in a rush."*

On this, the Pan Am captain saw KLM's landing lights coming dead at them through the fog.

Captain: *"There he is...look at him...that...that son-of-a-bitch is coming!"*

First Officer: *"Get off! Get off! Get off!"*

The Pan Am captain pushed the throttles up to full power and swung left in to the tall grass in a desperate attempt to clear the runway, but 747s are enormous beasts and slow to respond.

And everyone in the Pan Am cockpit ducked.

The KLM captain suddenly saw Pan Am right in front of him and frantically yanked at the stick, trying to get his plane up in the air, but the aircraft was slow to respond, as well, on account of it now carrying 55 tons of extra fuel. Nose pitched high, and over-rotated, the KLM tail dragged and left a 66-foot long scrape of metal on the runway, cracked the concrete, and dug a six-foot deep trench in places. For 300 meters KLM was airborne, then its landing gear and engines on its starboard wing sliced into the Pan Am fuselage, peeling off the top.

Nearly 100,000 liters of aviation fuel gushed out of KLM's ruptured tanks, drenching many of the Pan Am passengers in aviation fuel.

Pan Am's engines were still running full bore. First Officer, Robert Bragg, reached down to turn off the "start levers." He grabbed all four and pulled. Nothing happened. The controls to the engines had been severed. Bragg reached up to switch off the "fire handles." The fire handles are a group of four overhead switches that cut off the fuel supply, the hydraulics serving the engines, the air flow, and the electricity. Bragg looked up where the fire handles should be, but the top of the cockpit was missing, even the cockpit windows. Bragg turned, looked back and saw that the entire hump and top of the fuselage had been sheared off and he could see all the way back to the tail. There had been 28 passengers in the upper deck lounge and now the upper deck lounge was no longer there.

The fuselage was stressed and twisted to such a degree, all

emergency exits, except one, failed to open.

And the engines continued to run at full speed.

Passengers and crew seated aft of row 30 were already dead. Many passengers, who had survived the crash, simply sat frozen in their seats, in shock, deer in the headlights, unable to budge. They, too, would perish.

Some forty to fifty passengers fought through debris, fire and a melting fuselage, and escaped out onto a wing through a hole in the side of the aircraft. They were terrified to get anywhere near the roaring engines. And they were afraid to jump off the wing and down to the ground. It was a long drop, nearly two stories.

A woman finally jumped first. Other passengers followed her lead, but they landed on the woman, breaking her back, legs and arms.

There were horrible screams as the deer-in-the-headlights' passengers banged on windows. Then a horrific stench, the smell of burning flesh.

My classmate Carrie Thomas survived the crash and she was able to get that only exit open, the exit at L2. She managed to get passengers out and miraculously down to the ground.

There had been two Pan Am employees seated in the observer seats behind the pilots. They ended up hanging upside down by their seatbelts in First Class. They had to hold onto what was left of a wall, release their seatbelts and escape out a hole in the aircraft. Pan Am Captain Victor Grubbs, realizing that most of the cockpit floor was missing, jumped through it, landed in First Class and fell all the way through the First Class floor into the cargo hold. He was found by purser Dorothy Kelly under the jumbo on his hands and knees, stunned senseless. Dorothy Kelly had "seen something white" in the tall grass (the captain's Pan Am flight shirt) and she ran to help. Despite having a broken arm, she dragged dazed Captain Grubbs to safety and he survived.

There were a series of small explosions, then the inboard engine exploded and blew debris and large pieces of metal over Dorothy Kelly and Captain Grubb's heads. One of the shards of metal struck Carrie Thomas who had gone back to help an elderly gentleman who was struggling to get away from the aircraft.

Carrie was decapitated.

In that instant, the Pan Am jumbo listed and collapsed down onto its belly in the very spot where Dorothy Kelly had found Captain Grubbs in the tall grass.

Local Canarian citizens heard the explosions and rushed to the airport to help. They climbed over fences to get on airport property. Soon, airport authorities opened all gates to the airport to allow locals access. A radio call for help went out to everyone who resided in the area to drive onto the airport proper and help get survivors to hospitals. Due to the dense fog, airport employees and locals thought only one aircraft was involved and they hurried to the KLM crash site to see if there were any survivors.

It would be over twenty minutes before any emergency crews discovered that Pan Am was involved and finally came to their aid.

Back at the Pan Am crash site, First Officer Robert Bragg heard a noise behind him. He turned and was shocked to see a taxi pulling up. The taxi driver took charge and was instrumental in getting the seriously injured Bragg to the hospital.

All 248 (including six infants) aboard KLM perished. Seventy of the 396 from Pan Am emerged from the inferno alive. Most were badly burned. Nine of these survivors would later die from their injuries.

Carrie was gone and so were 582 others, in what is still known as the worst disaster in aviation history.

36

I Travel to Tenerife

As I pen these final pages regarding the crash, I'm actually on the island of Tenerife, in the seaside resort of Puerto de la Cruz. I'm 12 miles from where the accident took place. I've just been up there and this is what I saw. At the back of the airport was that perimeter fence the locals climbed over. I could easily see exit C-3 and exit C-4 which lead to the taxiway—and where the accident took place. Behind me stood an old ATC tower. It was small and only two stories high, left over from when the airport was first built.

Something protruding from the fence caught my eye. There were *still* plastic memorial flowers stuck in the fence. I looked up and down the uneven, undulating 11,000 foot runway. It is said, all these years later, airport workers are still finding on the grass strips boarding the taxiways, the odd nut or bolt or small fragment of metal from the two 747s.

No wonder, a 747 is made up of approximately six million parts.

I spoke to locals who live near the airport. They told me a chilling story. Nearby Santa Cruz is the largest city on the island of Tenerife. When it was determined that Tenerife needed an airport, they hired and engineer/airport architect to research where the best location to build an airport would be. He travelled all over the island making notes and maps. Since Santa Cruz is in the north, the north was obviously the first choice. For those of you who have been to Tenerife, you know there aren't many places in the north to build any airport. The geography is made up of mountains and volcanoes, cut by deep ravines called *barrancos*. The north of Tenerife looks like the island in the movie *King Kong*.

After exhaustive studies, the airport architect was ready to present his findings, but he died before a meeting could be arranged. A sophisticated map showing the most ideal places to build an airport was found amongst the deceased engineer's possessions. A big red X marked the spot where the airport was to be built. The spot was Los Rodeos, an area with the worst weather on the island.

The airport was built.

And only years later, did authorities discover, the big red X on the map was the singular place on the island where the engineer had felt NO AIRPORT SHOULD BE BUILT.

I left the airport behind and drove four miles up to a sheared off mountain—a "mesa." Indeed, it's called Mesa Mota, and it's where the Pan Am/KLM Memorial is located.

I stood in front of the towering memorial and searched the valley in front of me for the Los Rodeos airport. There were low-lying clouds and swirling fog, and I couldn't see anything which resembled an airport. Then, the clouds parted, and I saw below me what the cockpit crew of Pan Am Clipper *Victor* must have seen when they banked the jumbo and started their final approach. As quickly as the clouds had parted, they swept back in and swallowed the airport whole. I was startled how fast it closed down the airport.

Why build an airport here, indeed. What the hell were they thinking?

I said a prayer for Carrie and the crew and passengers on those two 747s, then I made my way back down from the mesa and headed for the dual carriageway that passes by the airport on my way back to Puerto de la Cruz. The airport was still socked in, but just a few miles away the island of Tenerife was basking in glorious wall-to-wall sun and I could see snow on the top of the volcano Mt. Teide.

Sun and clear skies everywhere.

Everywhere except for the airport.

37

A Change in the Air, and a Chill

The Tenerife disaster forced aviation authorities to insist on the use of *standard phrases*, as opposed to such colloquialisms as "OK" in radio responses. The phrase "take-off" is no longer used until the actual take-off. Instead, control towers and aircrew refer to "departure."

Ground radar has been installed at Los Rodeos.

* * *

Here are some chilling scenarios regarding the crash: Because of the thick fog, the control tower wasn't aware that there had been an accident until an aircraft circling overhead in a holding pattern spotted smoke, wreckage and fire down on the runway below. Indeed, the controllers had heard the explosion, but thought terrorists had blown up a fuel truck.

Remember my friend Susan Lovejoy? The flight attendant who first encouraged me to work for the airlines? Her best friend and new husband were on their honeymoon. They wanted to spend it doing something really romantic, so they decided on the Canary Islands. They were sitting in the upper deck lounge of Pan Am when KLM hit.

The accident happened just after 5pm, local, but the inferno was not extinguished until 3.30am the following day, 10½ hours later.

Five-thousand kilograms of foam and 500,000 liters of water were used to extinguish the fire.

There weren't enough caskets on the island of Tenerife to accommodate the 583 victims, and caskets had to be flown down from London.

That Dutch passenger Robina Van Lanschot who refused to re-board KLM and chose to stay behind? Remember her?

She married her boyfriend and they are still together to this day.

Los Rodeos airport has been renamed Tenerife *Aeropuerto del Norte*. New name, but the bad weather hasn't changed. Since being built, there have been over 1000 fatalities at the airport.

The football match that was on the portable radio in the control tower, finished eight minutes after the accident.

Before emergency crews arrived, witnesses reported seeing someone spirit a portable radio out of the control tower.

Many of the victims in the Pan Am Tenerife crash were elderly, and they were wearing dentures. Their dentures were never found, and their remains couldn't be formally identified. The advent of DNA testing did not come into practice until 1985, eight years later.

KLM had had enough fuel to make it back to Amsterdam. They hadn't needed to refuel.

EPILOGUE

Back home in Key West, Florida, I meet a gay couple from New York. I notice one of the women is wearing a gold necklace with a Pan Am logo. We talk. She tells me that when Pan Am collapsed in 1991, she was helping to empty offices and remove documents from filing cabinets. She "acquired" the official handwritten statements of three of the Pan Am employees who survived the crash in Tenerife: a flight attendant, a maintenance man who occupied a jump seat in the cockpit and First Officer Robert Bragg. I ask the woman if she would send me copies of the documents. She declines, fearing repercussions. I tell her I don't know who she is or where she lives. She still won't go for it. I give her my address in the hope she will change her mind. Months later, out of the blue, copies arrive in the mail.

It is from these statements, I was able to ascertain much of what transpired in the Canary Islands.

* * *

So as not to end on a somber note, might I just add that my days (and many long nights) with Pan Am were simply the very best of times. I made great friendships, which as you know, endure until this day and will last to the end of time.

I was blessed by having the opportunity to visit places that I had always dreamt about and equally so to visit many cities that I didn't even know existed. I fell in love with distant lands, and I often had the bejesus scared out of me along the way, which somehow made it all the more interesting.

Pan Am opened my eyes to new horizons and gave me a million things that I would never have had, never have been able to capture and experience all on my own in my lifetime.

Pan Am was an education. It was our graduate degree in foreign languages, sociology, psychology, culture and etiquette.

I would not trade those years with Pan Am for all the crude in the Tengiz oil field of Kazakhstan, all the coffee in the fertile soils of the Paraíba valleys of Brazil, or all the tea in the Lesser Himalayas of Darjeeling. And I didn't need to trade it for the world, for the world was our beckoning oyster.

There will never, ever, be another airline like Pan Am.

Pan Am—*we* were Pan Am, and that made us the luckiest souls on the face of the planet.

THE PAN AM LEGEND LIVES ON:

Visit the **Pan Am Historical Foundation**

And the **Pan Am Museum Foundation**

Bibliography

Daley, Robert—*An American Saga, Juan Trippe and His Pan Am Empire*, Random House, New York & Toronto, 1980

Bender, Marylin, and Altschul, Selig—*The Chosen Instrument: Pan Am, Juan Trippe, The Rise and Fall of an American Entrepreneur*, Simon & Schuster, New York, 1982

Davies, R.E.G.—*Pan Am, An Airline and Its Aircraft*, Crown, New York, 1987

Gandt, Robert—*Skygods, The Fall of Pan Am*, William Morrow, New York, 1995

Trippe, Betty Stettinius—*Pan Am's First Lady: The Diary of Betty Stettinius Trippe*, Paladwr Press, Virginia, 1996

Macintyre, Ben—*The Napoleon of Crime: The Life and Times of Adam Worth, Master Thief*, Broadway Books, Reprint edition New York, 2011

Okrent, Daniel—*Last Call: the Rise and Fall of Prohibition*, Scribner, New York, 2011

Riegel, Betty—*Up in the Air: The real story of life aboard the world's most glamorous airline*, Simon & Schuster UK, London, 2013

Made in the USA
Columbia, SC
01 June 2018